The Human Element

D0141571

The HUMAN ELEMENT

Understanding and Managing Employee Behavior

Lee Roy Beach

M.E.Sharpe
Armonk, New York
London, England

Library of Congress Cataloging-in-Publication Data

Beach, Lee Roy.
  The human element : understanding and managing employee behavior /
by Lee Roy Beach.
    p. cm.
Includes bibliographical references and index.
ISBN: 978-0-7656-2035-4 (cloth: alk. paper)—ISBN: 978-0-7656-2036-1 (cloth: alk. paper)
    1. Organizational behavior—Management. 2. Supervision of employees. 3. Problem solving.
I. Title. II. Title: Understanding and managing employee behavior.

HD58.7.B412 2007
658.4—dc22   2006038941

Printed in the United States of America

The paper used in this publication meets the minimum requirements of
American National Standard for Information Sciences
Permanence of Paper for Printed Library Materials,
ANSI Z 39.48-1984.

∞

BM (c)   10   9   8   7   6   5   4   3   2   1
BM (p)   10   9   8   7   6   5   4   3   2   1

To Byron Bissell, Margie Barber, and Barbara Beach,
from whom I have learned so much, with special thanks to
Linda Miller and James Wise for their help and good advice.

Contents

Preface

This book is for managers (and those about to become managers) who find themselves stressed and confused about how to deal with their employees.

With the possible exception of the military, which is a rather special world, it is common practice in modern organizations of all kinds to assign responsibility for employee management to people who have no idea how to do it. Even business school graduates find themselves overwhelmed despite having taken courses in human resources and, perhaps, supervision. This is largely because their courses focused more on legal and policy issues than on the day-to-day "people problems" that keep managers awake at night. Don't misunderstand me—knowing about legal and policy issues is crucial, it just isn't enough.

I wrote this book to supplement the important things that are taught in human resource and supervision courses. I am a psychologist by training, but I have been a professor and an administrator in a business school for a number of years, and I have done a good deal of research and consulting in a variety of organizations. The purpose of education is to pass on what one has learned through experience and mistakes, so those who follow don't have to start from scratch and can avoid the mistakes. This book is my way of passing on what I have learned.

The Human Element

1

Introduction

Whatever the term—my boss, my supervisor, my manager—nearly everyone in every organization reports to somebody who oversees their job performance. The CEO reports to the board of directors, the division heads report to the CEO, an administrative assistant reports to a division head, an office staff reports to an office manager, team members report to a team leader, assembly line workers report to a foreman. For convenience, we will refer to all of the people to whom others report as "managers," no matter what their job title may be, and we will refer to the people who report to them as their "employees."

Most managers are reasonably intelligent, generally well intended, appropriately self-confident, and technically competent, or they wouldn't be managers in the first place. However, even the most successful managers admit to great uneasiness when it comes to dealing with their employees' expectations, behavior, emotions, and performance problems. Over the course of our careers, most of us have lost more hours of sleep over issues related to our employees than over any other aspect of our jobs.

In contrast to the strategic and administrative aspects of managers' jobs, employee management focuses on individual workers, making sure that they have the resources, skills, and guidance they need to meet their own and the organization's expectations. Because the organization's overall effort is made up of the combined efforts of all of its employees, the quality of that overall effort depends upon good employee management to ensure that each worker's contribution is the best it can be.

Good employee management is not solely about efficiency and productivity. Every manager's job also includes a responsibility to work with individual employees to establish mutual expectations about their respective responsibilities and how they each will behave toward the other in order to create an

1

atmosphere that both enhances performance and builds commitment to the organization. Indeed, management of expectations is the key to successful employee management because expectations are the standards against which they, and you, judge everything that happens. When expectations are met, all is well. When expectations are not met, trouble ensues. Most management problems involving employees stem from conflicting expectations or from failures on the part of either the employees or their manager to meet the other's expectations.

Although employee management occurs at every level of the organization, surprisingly few people actually are taught how to do it. Most training programs are after-the-fact, remedial, and focus on specific problems, such as morale or interpersonal conflict. Moreover, most fail to recognize the centrality of expectation management to successful employee management. As a result, otherwise capable people find themselves thrust into employee management without a clue about what to do. Some find they have a natural talent for it and simply get on with the job. Some get good advice and learn fast enough to survive—but with sleepless nights. The rest flounder around until they develop some kind of expedient that reduces their anxiety while producing the illusion that they know what they're doing.

Some Expedients That Look Like Employee Management, But Aren't

Over the years, I have observed both good and bad employee managers and tried to figure out what makes them different. The bulk of this book is about what the good ones do. But, before we go there, let's look at some of the expedients the bad ones have adopted to cover up the fact that they don't know what they're doing. I'm sure I've missed a few, but these are some of the expedients that I've observed, repeatedly, and the problems that I've seen arise from their use.

Laissez-faire

As you know, laissez-faire means (roughly) "let them do as they will." As an expedient, the manager tries to be "hands off," and let the employees get on with things. This sounds admirably democratic, trusting, and empowering, but it works only when the employees really know their jobs, are exceptionally motivated and self-directed, and have unhindered access to information about what is wanted of them and why. Moreover, it assumes that their expectations about their performance coincide with management's, which is unlikely if their manager makes no effort to ensure that it happens.

In some organizations, primarily small ones involving professional people (like physicians, lawyers, or professors) or highly trained technicians, laissez-faire can work. Indeed, in these organizations it may be the only thing the manager can do without provoking a revolt; experts don't like to be told what to do, ever. But in large organizations or organizations with less motivated, less self-sufficient people, laissez-faire seldom works. If nothing else, information flow in large organizations seldom is what it should be, even with modern technology, and the manager plays a crucial role in transmitting requirements and perspective (expectations) from the organization to the individual workers. Failure to perform this basic function is bad enough, but if it is compounded by failure to provide resources, skills, and guidance, it is foolish to expect good results.

A major problem with laissez-faire is that employees have fairly clear expectations about what constitutes good employee management, and they become very unhappy when their manager falls short—and doing nothing usually falls short. As we shall see, one of the functions of a manager, at a minimum, is to coordinate the activities of all of his or her employees. If the manager refuses to do this, the employees must patch together ways of doing it themselves, which takes time and effort from their real jobs and arouses resentment for having to do what they expect the manager to do.

If employees are not self-sufficient or if they try to scam the system, laissez-faire won't work at all. Sad to say, some people need oversight if they are to behave well—they may have good intentions, but they somehow need to know somebody is paying attention to what they do, somebody who can reward or punish them, somebody who is available to help them if they have difficulties. Managers who fail these people are failed managers and soon will be replaced.

Let's Be Friends

This expedient is a variant on the laissez-faire expedient and often is motivated by fear of one's employees and a perceived need to defend one's self from them. The expectation is that the employees will be nice to you if you are their friend, so the expedient is to do whatever it takes to promote friendship. These managers invite employees to share confidences, and they share their own. They seek social contact outside the workplace. They try to be patient, uncritical, undemanding, and are willing to go the extra mile to avoid conflict or hurting someone's feelings.

Managers who use this expedient seldom realize that they are, in fact, attempting to put their employees in a corner: nice people are expected to be kind to their friends and do what their friends ask them to do. So, if the manager is their friend, employees should be nice and do what they are asked to do. However, this expedient can't work for long because not everybody will accept the premise: most employees know that they and the manager are not really friends, if only because they frequently have opposed interests. They know that the manager is the boss, whose interests are primarily aligned with those of the employer. The manager's job is to promote productivity, and this often involves pressing employees to behave in ways they otherwise wouldn't. Moreover, employees seldom are comfortable with friendship being forced on them and the falseness this entails. Because they don't believe the premise, they don't play by the rule—they don't feel constrained to be especially nice, and they don't feel obliged to do what they are asked to do.

Martinet

This expedient is the exact opposite of the laissez-faire and the let's be friends expedients and is often adopted by managers who are afraid of their employees, but in this case they assume that the best defense is a good offense. They mistake severity and inflexibility for strength and think that issuing orders is the same as communicating. They behave as though they have nothing but contempt for their employees—in some cases they do; in others it is mere defensiveness. They expect to prevail if they stay on top of everything, hoard important information, subjugate their employees, and use their power like a cudgel. They usually expect that their employees are slackers who want to avoid work and will goof off if not watched every minute. They seldom give good performance reviews, and they use threat of verbal abuse, outright punishment, or being fired as a way of ensuring obedience.

The martinet expedient is never expedient for long. Employees will leave if they can, and, whether they stay or not, they will tell tales about how badly they are treated. Worse, they will actively sabotage the manager's efforts, if only in little ways that have a cumulative effect. They usually are still there after the manager has been transferred, demoted, or fired.

Rule Maker

This expedient is used by managers who aspire to be martinets but can't quite bring it off. They settle for acting like they're on top of things by issuing an endless stream of memos, most of which contain new rules. Somebody knocks over a vase of flowers—a memo comes out banning flowers. Somebody leaves work ten minutes early—a memo appears banning early departures. Somebody wears shorts to work—a memo is issued banning shorts. They're always behind the curve, making up rules for things that already happened, things that are better handled by dealing with the individuals involved than by imposing yet another rule on everybody, and things that often are so petty that they don't matter anyway. After a while nobody can keep track of all the rules, including the manager. The result is that the rules aren't enforced, which makes them both useless and laughed-at.

A profusion of useless, laughed-at rules is worse than no rules at all because they foster a lack of respect for the rules that really count (and make it hard to tell which ones count). It's like the boy who kept crying "Wolf!" when there was no wolf; nobody took him seriously when he yelled it just before he was eaten. The manager who keeps making up arbitrary, toothless rules loses credibility. This undermines sensible rules because nobody knows which ones are sensible or whether the manager actually means for them to be obeyed.

Rules exist for only one purpose, to limit people's freedom of action. Therefore, they shouldn't be imposed without reason. The only legitimate reason for rules in the workplace is to establish standards for how employees are expected to behave in order to enhance performance. Usually, arbitrary, ad hoc rules lack legitimacy and merely confuse things, because they are tangential to performance. They don't even convey the impression of being in control that the manager is striving to create.

Cult Leader

This expedient is an exaggerated version of the let's be friends expedient, with a little bit of martinet thrown in and is often adopted by managers who want to insulate themselves against real or perceived threats by other managers or their own bosses. They strengthen their position by promoting what might be called a "personality cult." That is, they strive to make their employees so loyal to them as an individual that personal threats become threats to the group as a whole. Their strength lies in the unwillingness of outsiders to do anything that would prompt the group to retaliate by withholding service or rendering slow or flawed service. I once saw a computer tech-support group hold an entire organization hostage to its manager's whims (and his budget demands) by simply slowing down their responses to his "enemy's" technical support requests.

Employees can become almost blindly loyal to their managers, even managers they don't like, when they expect that their own security and prosperity depend on the manager's efforts. Every manager runs interference for his or her employees, but when this is seen as somehow heroic in the face of daunting obstacles, ties of loyalty become strong. The downside for the individual cult members is that any hint of disloyalty, through failure to follow orders or by questioning a position adopted by the manager, places them in jeopardy.

Disloyalty makes the person a social outcast, prompts poor performance evaluations by the cult leader, reduces claims on rewards reaped by the group, and can lead to actual expulsion from the group, although dissenters tend to get out before they are driven out. In short, once the individual is locked into the cult, there is no room for dissent—there's no way but the manager's way.

From the manager's viewpoint, the cult expedient has two gigantic flaws: insiders are fickle, and outsiders distrust and resent cults. Insiders start to defect when they realize their expectations can't be met—the manager isn't superhuman and can't always deliver the promised levels of security and prosperity. Once defections begin, the whole thing starts to unravel and the manager quickly loses leverage. Outsiders distrust cults because they are dedicated to the cult leader's interests, not the organization's. They resent cults because cults usually are bullies. Those who are bullied often join together to undermine the cult, meaning that in addition to unrelenting efforts to retain employee loyalty, the manager has to fight off plots by outsiders. Few managers can sustain this level of effort. Eventually something goes wrong and defections or plots bring the cult down, leaving the manager unprotected and unable to work with either the betrayed insiders or the outraged outsiders.

Divide and Conquer

This expedient leads to something like a cult, but without the loyalty. It involves subtly pitting employees against each other so that the manager is the only person each of them trusts. This is a difficult expedient to execute successfully, but when you see it done by a master, it's hard not to admire the sheer audacity. I knew an office manager who used this expedient because she was not as well trained, as bright, or as talented as her employees. Her scheme was simple, but she executed it brilliantly. She withheld information, which kept everybody off balance. She fostered gossip and rumors, which kept them distrustful of each other. She attributed her more outrageous actions to orders from her boss, which made her appear blameless for all the bad things that kept happening and even allowed her to "protect" favored employees from the imaginary wrath of that evil boss. But, most effective of all, she gave overlapping tasks to different people, leading them to expect rewards and punishments based on performance, and then acted as the arbitrator when things became muddled and turf wars broke out. By keeping her employees off balance and at each others' throats, she could ward off challenges to her authority and appear to be the voice of reason. Of course, turnover was high, morale was low, paranoia was rampant, conflict was the norm, and efficiency was nearly nonexistent. Employees were reduced to competing for her approval, like children trying to please a parent. Although the carnage was unbelievable, the manager regarded herself as a success. And, because she was so cunning, her boss could never build a sufficient case for removing her. She's retired now, but when I think of all her former employees, I somehow imagine all these pathetic, shattered wrecks, withdrawn from the world with only cats and bitterness to comfort them.

Trustees

This expedient is a variation of the divide and conquer expedient. Instead of setting all employees against each other, this expedient creates an elite subgroup of employees and gives them special privileges and duties. (The analogy is with the trustees in a jail, who receive special treatment and who help oversee their fellow prisoners.) The members of the elite become unofficial "assistant managers" whose interests are aligned with the manager's and who therefore can be trusted. By delegating authority to the elite, the manager creates an illegitimate but powerful new level of supervision between him or her and the majority of the employees, often eliminating most of his or her direct contact with them.

Like the previous expedients, the trustee expedient seldom works for long. The non-elite employees usually hate this "some-folks-are-more-equal-than-other-folks" arrangement. When they become sufficiently outraged, the non-elites become subversive, engaging in sabotage and tattling to higher management. Once higher management learns about the manager's ad hoc creation of a new managerial level and wholesale delegation of his or her duties, they usually feel obliged to destroy it—after all, the manager is being paid to manage the employees, not create a little empire.

Let's Make a Deal

Finally, the most common expedient adopted by ill-trained managers is to make all dealings with employees into semi-economic transactions. Over time, an unstated but surprisingly explicit contract evolves between the manager and the employees. If they do their jobs and treat the manager well, they expect to receive specific rewards—praise, awards, bonuses, time off, and other privileges—everything is tit-for-tat. Sometimes the rewards are so predictable that they essentially are the employee's price list for doing the various aspects of his or her job. And, if the price isn't paid, performance suffers because the manager has violated the implicit contract.

The major downside of deal-making is that a pricing system makes everything rigid. Employees are unlikely to show much creativity or innovation, because no price has been established for anything new. It is easier and safer to stick with the status quo. Jobs therefore become sclerotic, unchanging, and dull. In effect, everyone's job degenerates into mere piecework; "do X, receive Y," time after time after time.

Unwillingness to be innovative can turn a mere crisis into an utter disaster. If employees don't know whether they will be rewarded or punished if they use their own judgment to deal with crises, crises simply don't get dealt with—"It's not my job."

When everything is a transaction, even routine changes resulting from shifts in the organization's overall strategy must be negotiated. Having to make a deal with each employee's expectations for every new activity is time consuming because each new activity's price has to be equivalent to or better than the price for a comparable old activity, and it isn't always clear what constitutes comparability. By and large, nothing gets done while the negotiation plays out, which slows everything down.

That is the end of my list of expedients, and I'm sure I haven't got them all. I've seen variations on each of them, and I've known managers whose truly appalling behavior doesn't fit any of them, but this litany of malfeasance should suffice.

Lessons Learned

The first lesson to be learned from expedients is that they don't work, at least not for long. And trying to make them work takes far more effort and generates far more anxiety than is involved in doing things right in the first place. They are just what the name implies, expedients—they are patches on the employee management problem, not solutions.

The second lesson is that most expedients are laced with cynicism and defensiveness, which creates a poisonous work environment for everyone, manager and employees alike. Managers who resort to expedients start by expecting employees to be dangerous, lazy, or stupid. They use deceit as a matter of course. They seek to manipulate rather than motivate. They play to the employees' weaknesses rather than their strengths. You can't expect anything good to come from so much that is bad.

The third lesson is that expedients are more about power than about management. Their goal is to give the manager power over others or to build defensive walls to protect him or her from the power of others—employees, other managers, or the manager's bosses. This means that the expedients are really about the manager, about meeting his or her expectations, rather than about establishing mutual expectations aimed at accomplishing whatever tasks the group has been assigned. This is their greatest flaw. The organization cannot tolerate failure to get things done—it causes trouble for everyone else, and it impedes progress toward the organization's goals. Failed, or even impaired, performance has consequences, usually replacement of the manager.

I suppose some managers graduate from expedients to being good employee managers as their anxiety decreases and their good sense kicks in. This must be true or there would be far fewer successful managers than there actually are. I suspect that feedback from bosses, peers, and employees whips most of us into shape in the long run. However, it would be so much easier if we started out with the necessary knowledge, rather than having to learn it in the school of hard knocks. Life is too short for fumbling toward knowledge that other people already possess and are willing to share.

Just as I have observed bad managers, I have observed good ones and I've tried to figure out what they do that makes them good. At first I could see no discernable pattern because each of them does what is required by their particular circumstances. But, when I stepped back and looked at the larger picture, it became clear that whatever else they may value, good managers value superior employee performance most. Indeed, supervision exists primarily to help employees do their best, thereby ensuring that the unit and the organization do their best. Managers have many functions (administrator, teacher, counselor, perhaps even parent), but ultimately their success is judged by their employees' and their unit's success in promoting the organization's success. Good managers make sure this happens by accepting six prime commitments.

Good Managers' Six Commitments

- *Leadership.* Good managers commit to actively leading their employees.
- *Expectations.* Good managers commit to understanding their own and their employees' work-related expectations and how they affect behavior.
- *Emotions.* Good managers commit to anticipating the emotions that arise from threatened or violated expectations and to dealing with them constructively.
- *Standards.* Good managers commit to translating their expectations about how employees should behave into clear performance standards.
- *Problems.* Good managers commit to carefully evaluating the problems that arise when their own and their employees' expectations are not met.
- *Solutions.* Good managers commit to solving problems that arise from unmet expectations promptly, fairly, and effectively.

The Plan

This book is about how to meet each of these six commitments. The following chapters will examine each of these commitments, describing the actions required to meet them.

2

Leading Employees

Good managers commit to actively leading their employees.

Managerial Units

Before we begin, we must be clear about what we mean when we talk about "you and your employees" as an entity—an entity that we will call a "managerial unit," or just "unit" for short. Throughout our discussion *a managerial unit is defined as one manager and one or more employees who report directly to that manager.*

For example, the Head of Accounting would be the manager of a unit made up of herself and the heads of the various divisions of her department, all of whom report directly to her. These division heads would, in turn, be managers of the employees who report directly to them. Further, one of these direct reports might manage a team tasked with gathering information for the annual report, which would constitute yet another unit, and so on down the line. Of course, a manager may manage more than one unit; the department head may manage the division heads as one unit and, at the same time, manage a unit consisting solely of herself and an administrative assistant. From this point of view, the box labeled "Accounting" in the organization chart doesn't designate a single entity. Rather, it represents all the managerial units that make up the accounting function of the organization.

In practice, most managers regard their units as larger than merely themselves and their direct reports. They regard anyone for whom they are responsible, however indirectly, as part of their unit. Formally, this is correct; they are responsible for everyone in their box in the organizational chart. But even with the flattened organizations of recent times, it usually is the case that most of the people in that box report to someone who reports to someone and so on, up to the person at the top of the box. Additionally, there are two compelling arguments for our more limited definition of a unit:

- Employees usually regard the person to whom they report as their boss. The person to whom their boss reports is regarded as their boss's boss. Most employees respect this difference, regarding it as inappropriate to report to their boss's boss unless specifically invited to do so and with their own boss's knowledge.
- Employees' work-related contact is almost exclusively with their own boss, their own peers, and their own direct reports. They seldom have much work-related contact with their boss's boss, their peers' bosses, or their peers' employees, or with employees who report to their direct reports.

The reason for insisting on talking about units, and for insisting on our definition of them, is to avoid talking as though "manager" always means the person at the top of the box. Rather, we want to talk about everyone who is charged with direct, close collaboration with a limited number of employees for whom he or she is primarily responsible. Hence we define a unit as a manager (anywhere in the box) and the employees who report directly to him or her. The advantage of this way of thinking is quite straightforward: the human element in managing employees is pretty much the same anywhere in the organization—within boxes, at the top of boxes, clear up to the highest box on the chart.

The Maintenance/Change Decision

Each unit has a prescribed role within the set of units to which it belongs (e.g., the various units that comprise the Accounting Department), and the manager's job is to ensure that the unit plays its role successfully. To do so, the manager must decide whether the unit requires maintenance or change. A unit that has a well-defined task with equally well-defined procedures for accomplishing that task, where everyone knows what to expect, and that is humming along with no complaints and no pressures to do anything more or anything differently, may merely require maintenance. However, a unit that is under pressure to change expectations, to do more or do it differently as the organization responds to a dynamic world, requires constant change. Maybe the change isn't always big, and maybe it is gradual, but it still is change.

Frankly, if you decide on maintenance, you probably ought to get another job. If your organization isn't changing to meet its evolving environment, it probably is becoming geriatric and won't be around long anyhow. If the organization is changing, but you don't think your unit has to change too, you probably aren't going to be around long around either. Either way, you should be looking for work.

If, however, you decide on change, however small and however gradual, you, as manager of your unit, must take the lead in those changes. Leading begins with learning about the organization, its vision, strategy, and culture, and the role your unit plays in its pursuit of its goals. Then, on the basis of what you learn, you must work with your employees to design and implement changes that enable the unit to perform its role as well as it possibly can. At the same time, you must now learn about the human element—about yourself and your employees—so you can build on your collective strengths and fix, or work around, your collective weaknesses to create a unit that is the best that it can be. This is a task worth undertaking. And note how much it differs from mere maintenance, where the manager may be reduced to coercion, acting as an "enforcer" for the organization in order to keep employees in line.

The Unit as a Mini-Enterprise

Focusing on the manager as the active leader of a unit within a group of related units allows us to view each unit as a mini-enterprise embedded in a network of other mini-enterprises. Each mini-enterprise's (each unit's) operating environment is shaped by the demands and constraints imposed by its cooperation and competition with other units in the network (some of which are its suppliers and customers), as well as the larger organization's business strategy and, as we shall see, its culture. Like any enterprise, the unit must leverage its strengths and mitigate its weaknesses as it strives to reach its goals in the context of the threats and opportunities within its operating environment. Of course, a unit is not a thing, it is a group of people, and it doesn't really have a mind with which to appraise goals, strengths, weaknesses, threats, or opportunities. Neither does it have expectations that provide motivation to strive, nor understanding that provides direction for action. It is the people in the group who have to do the thinking and expecting and acting—you and your employees working together, with you as leader.

The Leader's Job

In any enterprise, whatever its size, the leader's job is to formulate an overall picture (a vision) that helps the employees of the enterprise understand its environment and the goals that follow from its struggle to survive and prosper within that environment. Then, in collaboration with the employees, the leader is responsible for formulating a strategic plan for attaining the enterprise's goals, implementing that plan, and monitoring its progress toward the goals—altering course to fit changing conditions. These same tasks, in essence, fall to every manager who leads a unit.

Of course, there is a difference between leading a whole organization and leading a managerial unit within that organization. The unit's leader operates on a much reduced scale with a much reduced set of options—but on a much more personal level with the people whose efforts are actually moving the organization forward. It is this human element that makes unit management so tough, and so interesting. Indeed, even though units usually are small and their roles, processes, and procedures are narrowly defined, the fact that they involve direct, often quite intense, human interactions makes unit management arguably the most difficult part of every manager's job. Unlike the organization's leaders' grand plans and brilliant strategies, unit leadership involves few abstractions and lots of practicalities—failure at this level bodes poorly for the organization's success at any level, so good unit management is the foundation upon which the organization' pursuit of survival and prosperity is built.

To be successful as the leader of your unit, you must:

- Learn about your unit's operating environment within the larger organization—including the organization's culture;
- Articulate your unit's role within that operating environment as well as the goals it must pursue as part of that role;
- Articulate a vision encompassing those goals and setting expectations for the future—"What are we now and what do we want to become?"
- Formulate a plan for accomplishing the goals and attaining the vision;
- Appraise the threats to and opportunities for goal attainment within your unit's environment;
- Appraise your unit's strengths and weaknesses in relation to goal attainment within that environment;
- Formulate strategies aimed at thwarting threats, taking advantage of opportunities, mitigating weaknesses, and leveraging strengths in pursuit of your unit's goals;
- Coordinate your own and your employees' expectations to facilitate successful implementation of the plan—make sure everyone is "reading off the same page."

An Example

To make this concrete, imagine that you are the head of the Cataloging Department in the research library of a very large museum. The museum is a very old institution with a highly respected tradition of scholarship. Despite its large endowment, financial pressures forced it to open its doors to the public in 1982. Prior to that, it was strictly a research center, and its extensive library was, and is, a major contributor to its outstanding reputation. Newcomers quickly sense nostalgia for the old days before having had to "go public," and a fierce commitment to maintaining the museum's scholarly identity. Indeed, the library remains off-limits to any but the most distinguished scholars with the most impressive credentials, and the staff is wholly dedicated to providing the best possible service to these god-like beings.

The library is headed by the Librarian, and there are five departments: Receiving, Binding, Cataloging, Lending, and Administration. You and the other four department heads report directly to the Librarian, and each of you manages a small department of four to twenty people, each of whom is a direct report. That is, because there are no managerial layers within the departments, each department is, according to our definition, a single managerial unit.

Cataloging, your unit, has three different kinds of jobs: Runners, Catalogers, and Stackers. Runners transport books from Receiving and from Binding to the Catalogers, and take cataloged books to holding stations in the stacks where Stackers sort and shelve them. Upon receiving books from Runners, Catalogers determine the Library of Congress number for each book (which requires far more judgment and skill than is generally realized), mark the spine and inside of the book, and insert a coded electronic strip; then they enter all relevant information about the book into the computerized inventory and retrieval system. Stackers both shelve the books and manage the shelf space in the stacks, moving large sections of books to accommodate new books when things get crowded. After the books are shelved, they become the responsibility of the Lending Department, which retrieves books from the stacks and checks them out to the library's customers, the researchers; it also re-shelves the books when they are returned. The library has begun to build an e-book collection, and your department recently has hired a woman to help your Catalogers learn to deal with it. She is a computer jock rather than a traditional "library person" and has yet to become an accepted member of the unit.

Your unit always has a flow of incoming and outgoing work, but there are spurts that cause things to back up. On the one hand, Receiving gets shipments in bursts and Binding often waits until it has processed a large number of books before passing them on to Cataloging. On the other hand, competition among the Catalogers gets out of hand, resulting in a flood of (often inaccurately cataloged) books being sent to the Stackers, who react to the flood by ratcheting up their competition about who can shelve the most books in a day, resulting in improperly shelved books, which are essentially lost until someone happens across them and shelves them properly. All of this causes trouble for the Lending Department because requests for the backed-up books cannot be filled and the department cannot make accurate estimates of when the books will become available, and improperly shelved books can't be located to be loaned. As a result, backups lead to constant complaints from the head of the Lending Department and, if things get really bad, from the Librarian and even the Director of the museum. Of course, all of this reflects badly on your unit and upon you as a manager.

The Cataloging Department's operating environment is defined by the demands and constraints imposed by both the museum and the library—as well as by the other departments of the library. The demands and constraints imposed by the museum are for the library to serve researchers well, within the budget set for it. The demands and constraints imposed by the library are for the departments to function smoothly and as cost-effectively as possible so it can meet the museum's expectations for service and budget restraint. Both of these sets of demands and constraints compete with those imposed by the other departments in the library. If Receiving is slow in unpacking and recording deliveries, your unit's work is slowed. Similar problems arise if Binding suddenly finishes repair work on a chunk of a bequeathed private library (the library's major source of old and rare books), suddenly flooding your unit with additional work. Moreover, your unit is in the final stages of converting the books in the old part of the library's massive collection from the Dewey decimal system to the Library of Congress system—an ongoing and time-consuming process that comes to a stop whenever the workload peaks. This makes all the books that have been removed from the stacks for re-cataloging unavailable to researchers until the Catalogers can get back to work on them. Finally, the library's decision to build an electronic collection requires a different set of cataloging skills than your unit has previously used, hence the new technician, and your Catalogers must take time off to get the proper training, which, in effect, reduces your workforce and slows your work. In short, although your unit's role is narrowly defined and its procedures and processes are fairly limited, it has its share of difficulties.

Let us assume that you, as head of the Cataloging Department, decide that rather than just coping with things as they come, in an attempt to simply get by, you want to lead your unit in proactively seeking solutions to its problems. You begin by taking a cool, objective look at your unit's role in its operating environment and quickly see that it boils down to getting books into the collection so researchers can use them. From this you formulate a simple but necessary vision—which, for a small unit such as yours, is essentially a mission statement:

- Our job is to promptly and accurately catalog books so they are rapidly available to researchers.

From this you determine that the unit's goals are:

- Efficient throughput of both traditional books and e-books, which requires
  - Promptness
  - Accuracy

Achieving these goals requires a plan of action, and that plan requires you to examine your operating environment as well as the unit itself:

- Who are our suppliers?
  - Receiving
  - Binding
- Who are our customers?
  - Lending
- Who are the stakeholders?
  - The museum
  - The Librarian
  - The other departments (units)
  - The researchers

Then you must examine your unit's role within this operating environment and ask yourself if what you are doing serves your vision. If it doesn't, what can you change to make it serve the vision?

- What is our present system for obtaining books from Receiving?
  - How can it be made more efficient?
  - How can we work with them to avoid backlogs and other irregularities in the workflow?
- What is our present system for obtaining books from Binding?
  - How can it be made more efficient?
  - How can we work with them to avoid backlogs and other irregularities in the workflow?
- What is our present system for retrieving incorrectly or archaically (Dewey) cataloged books for re-cataloging?
  - How can it made more efficient?
- What is our present system for cataloging and re-cataloging books?
  - How can it be made more efficient?
- Are there appropriate new technologies that we should incorporate into our work?
- What changes in our present systems and the management of our workflow are necessitated by the library's goal of building an e-book collection?

- What are the training implications of the answers to all of these questions?
- What are the costs of any changes we propose to make and how do we finance them?
  - Cost cutting
  - Budget requests

The answers to these questions provide you with a list of action items, the nitty-gritty tasks that must be accomplished if the unit is to move toward achieving its vision of prompt and accurate cataloging of the library's printed and electronic books. Arranged in a logical order, usually along a timeline indicating when each task should begin and end, this list forms the basis of a plan. Augmented by details about how necessary skills and resources will be acquired for accomplishment of each task, the nascent plan becomes a full-fledged plan and implementation can begin.

A word about plans: things seldom turn out the way you thought they would. In fact, the plan probably is obsolete even before you begin its implementation. The unit's operational environment isn't static, so the plan can't be either. As implementation unfolds, you have to carefully monitor the effects of what you are doing and make adjustments so that you continue toward realization of the vision. A rigid plan in a changing world is bound to fail; the key to success is flexibility and good sense.

Collaboration

We've been talking as though you alone were doing all the work of evaluating the environment, framing the vision, deriving the goals, and designing the plan. You can do it all, of course, but you just make it harder on yourself when you try to get buy-in from your employees. You can save yourself the trouble of being Super-Manager and formulating the whole thing yourself, as well as the trouble of being Super-Salesperson and having to get buy-in from your employees (and probably get better results overall) by including your employees in the process from the beginning.

Research shows that people more readily accept a vision and the plan to achieve it when they have had a hand in building it—largely because they know what is expected of them, what is expected of their coworkers, what to expected as the plan is implemented, and what to expect if the plan succeeds or fails.

Because most units are relatively small, it often is possible to include everyone in this process. If the unit is too large, it is best to have the employees select a few coworkers to represent them in doing the work.

(Keep in mind, however, that time spent on this is time taken away from the regular work; if your unit is already at capacity, it may be too much to ask employees to do this too. Indeed, even if you do it all yourself, you may have to do it on your own time rather than fall behind in your work. But, for the sake of argument, let's assume there is enough slack to allow you and your employees to devote work time to formulating a vision and plan for your unit.)

If only because you've decided to be a leader, it is likely that you will have given a good deal of thought to what needs to be done before you bring your employees into it, which is both good and bad. It is good because you can cut the initial wandering about that is typical of any group trying to discuss a difficult issue. It is bad because you may either structure the discussion to reach the conclusions you already think are right, or you may become so wedded to your own take on things that you can't recognize the potential value of alternative views.

Everyone thinks they are good at conducting group discussions, and hardly anyone actually is (see Box 2.1). Most of us err on the side of dominating the meeting and pushing for the conclusions we favor. We usually tell ourselves that we want the discussion to be orderly and to the point—which may be true, but it also helps us stay in control. This is unfortunate because the magic of group discussions often lies in the unexpected, the offbeat, and what at first glance may look slightly crazy. Therefore, it is best to let others talk and to promote a little playfulness, within reason. You've got to keep the one or two most vocal individuals from dominating things, and playfulness mustn't evolve into a party, but short of this, you need to keep things loose—at least at first.

Let's return to you as Head of the Cataloging Department. You are gathering your employees together to form a vision and a plan for your unit. (And, in the course of doing so, build expectations that will work for, rather than against, acceptance of the plan and willing participation in its implementation.) Although your unit is small, this may require more than one meeting, so you should propose that the discussion take place in four segments, perhaps with a meeting for each segment.

- The first segment is *idea generation,* loosely guided by the questions you've already formulated (above), but allowing plenty of freedom for new ideas to emerge and be discussed.
- The second segment is *idea sorting:* the ideas are clustered together on the basis of their mutual relevance.
- The third segment is *idea consolidation:* the clusters of ideas are ordered in a logical way to produce the vision and the plan.

- This may consist of the tasks we know we must do and the tasks we have to research before we decide what to do.
- All of the known tasks should be arrayed on a timeline so that the order of implementation starts to emerge.
- As research results in decisions about the remaining tasks, they should be added to the timeline and appropriate revisions made to accommodate them.
- The fourth segment is *document preparation.*
  - The final timeline should be cleaned up, and a member of the group (perhaps you, or you and one other person) should be assigned the job of writing a document that begins with the vision, followed by the plan.
  - The document should be submitted to all of the discussants and another meeting held to iron out the details.
  - The revised document should be distributed to everyone in the unit, as well as to your boss, for criticism and correction.
  - The final document should be distributed and frequently consulted as implementation begins.

The document need not be lengthy—the museum's vision statement and related strategic plan may run to volumes, but yours need only be a few pages. Besides, nobody will read anything that's very long-winded, so keep it basic.

After everybody has signed off on the vision and the plan, it is time to assign responsibility for each of the tasks in the plan to the employees of the unit—including you. Each assignment must include a start date and a completion date, as well as specification of what will constitute successful completion of the task. Continuing with our library example, if two of the employees from the Cataloging Department are assigned responsibility for evaluating the unit's existing procedures for obtaining books from the Receiving Department and proposing changes, they must be told when to start their work and when it should be completed. In addition, they must be told that a concrete, detailed description of the current procedures must be produced and concrete, detailed descriptions of proposed changes must be submitted, along with explicit reasons for the proposed changes, including expected costs and benefits. When they have done their work, the group as a whole (or the sub-group serving as a committee) must decide if the proposed changes make sense and assign responsibility for making them. If money is needed, it is up to you to find it in your budget or make an effort to get additional funding from your boss or whoever controls resources.

This probably all sounds very complicated, unnecessarily so. But it isn't.

Box 2.1
How to Run a Meeting

There are three kinds of meetings: Business meetings, aimed at making decisions; discussion meetings, aimed at generating ideas; and negotiation meetings, aimed at reconciling conflicting interests. We will discuss negotiations in Chapter 8. The following are rules for running a business or a discussion meeting.

General Rules

1. **Plan ahead.** Send all participants a copy of the agenda or a statement of the issue to be discussed a few days before the meeting; include the date, time, and location of the meeting.
2. **Select a venue that is comfortable and without distractions;** refreshments, particularly beverages, are a good idea if put on a side table where getting them doesn't distract from the meeting. Business meetings can be set up in rows or around a table, with the leader in front of the group or at the head of the table. Discussion groups should be seated in a circle so the leader is less set apart from the group.
3. **Arrange for one group member to be the "scribe,"** who takes notes and watches the time; most meetings should be an hour or less, with the option of extending the time if necessary. Members should keep the hour following the meeting free in case it runs over the allotted time.
4. **Open the meeting with a review of the last meeting** and a statement about the goal(s) of this meeting.
5. **Establish ground rules for the meeting.**
   - ✓ One speaker at a time.
   - ✓ No side conversations.
   - ✓ Everyone gets a chance to speak.
   - ✓ All serious ideas are acceptable, but frivolous ones are not.
   - ✓ Criticism of ideas and proposals is acceptable; personal criticism of those who propose them is not.
6. **Establish ground rules for yourself** (but you needn't tell anyone else).
   - ✓ Don't talk too much; the point is dialogue not monologue.
   - ✓ Don't try to control everything; sometimes good emerges from messiness.
   - ✓ Be open to new ideas and viewpoints; you don't know it all.
   - ✓ Encourage shy people to talk; just because they're shy doesn't mean they've nothing valuable to contribute.

✓ Discourage those who tend to talk too much by regulating how often they have the floor, even if they're brilliant; excessive brilliance can be tedious.

Business Meetings

✓ Proceed through the agenda in an orderly manner, preferably following Robert's Rules of Order or a similar parliamentary procedure, if only informally.

✓ Start with easy, non-contentious items, to establish a sense of unity, and then move to the harder issues.

✓ Make it clear that criticism of ideas and proposals is acceptable, but criticism of persons is not.

✓ Have clear rules for decision making; consensus, majority vote, sense of the meeting, etc.

✓ Strive to reach decisions in the meeting; if this isn't possible, make sure that a mechanism is created to keep the issue alive—perhaps a person or a committee to look into it and make a recommendation at the next meeting.

✓ When a decision requires action, designate the person or persons responsible for doing it and set a deadline.

✓ Don't adjourn before reaching an agreement about the date and time of the next meeting.

✓ Follow up by issuing minutes of the meeting to all interested parties with a memo about the topic of the next meeting.

Discussion Meetings

✓ Open the discussion by asking for general thoughts on the issue under consideration, asking for comments on each idea, and steering clear of premature discussion of solutions or actions.

✓ Make sure that all plausible global issues are brought up before the discussion turns to more concrete considerations; otherwise entire areas of potential interest may never be considered.

✓ Allow the discussion to drift in unexpected ways; no order is needed at this stage.

✓ All serious ideas are acceptable; hold off on criticism until ideas are being sorted and screened.

✓ Write all ideas and related thoughts in clusters on a blackboard or on large sheets of paper located so everyone can see them.

- ✓ Don't let your discomfort with silence make you rush things; allow "dead time" so people can think. If this begins to degenerate into discussions irrelevant to the present issue, bring the focus back.
- ✓ Encourage people to address comments to each other, rather than just to you, but discourage side conversations that can detract from the main discussion.
- ✓ Try to play down your own role in the group, while maintaining a guiding hand.
- ✓ If people address their comments to you, do not look at them, look at other group members to encourage the speaker to address them, rather than you.
- ✓ If members ask you a question for other than factual information that you alone possess, turn to the others in the group for answers.
- ✓ It is the leader's job to decide when things have been discussed enough and redundancy is beginning to set in.
- ✓ Summarize the current state of the group's thinking when an issue has been discussed enough, but don't firm things too much; mushiness is acceptable in the early stages because subsequent meetings are to screen ideas, develop surviving ideas more thoroughly, and formulate action plans.

Units usually are small, and the scope of their actions is limited, so the vision is modest and the plan is reasonably simple. Nonetheless, going through this process will produce buy-in, because the buyers are also the sellers, and it ensures that everyone is in agreement—"reading off the same page"—as implementation proceeds. Moreover, going through this process together tends to produce a sense of unity among the participants, which promotes further cooperation and teamwork.

Culture

Earlier, we said that the unit's operating environment was shaped by the larger organization's business strategy and culture. We have talked a bit about the business strategy part of this, and now we turn to the culture part. Every organization has a culture, which consists of the core values and beliefs shared by the employees of the organization. Every unit has a culture that incorporates much of the organization's culture and has additional characteristics unique to the unit.

In our Cataloging Department example, the museum's and library's culture were only briefly described: the museum values its tradition of and reputation for scholarship, and is nostalgic for its pre-public days. The library takes pride in its role in the museum's success, in its own exclusivity, and in the service it renders to renowned scholars. No doubt their cultures are richer than we can know without further investigation, but the point is that you must understand them because they are a source of many of the demands and constraints to which your unit must respond. They constrain what you can do in pursuit of your unit's vision (every aspect of the plan must focus on service improvement) as well as your unit's vision itself (it must be congruent with the museum's conservative view of itself and it must be designed to enhance the museum's scholarly reputation).

Your unit's culture augments the organization's culture, giving the unit its uniqueness and individuality. Say, for example, that in contrast to Receiving, which wholly lacks a sense of urgency, your unit reflects the museum's culture in valuing service, which makes it prize productivity, and believes that competition among employees, in terms of number of books cataloged in a week, promotes productivity. Your culture generates enthusiasm and action, while Receiving's culture generates . . . something else.

Both organizational and unit cultures dictate shared expectations about how employees should be treated, how they should treat each other, and a host of other things that help shape the work-lives of everyone (see Box 2.2). If these expectations are met, everything is fine. If they are exceeded, people are pleased. But, if the expectations are violated (or even thought to have been violated), the negative reaction can be immense.

Cultural values and beliefs are reflected in the things the organization or unit honors and the things it censures, the morals of the stories its employees tell about its founders and other heroes, and the conventions to which its employees spontaneously and voluntarily adhere.

Values

Values are just that—the things that the culture endorses as meritorious in and of themselves or because they lead to other things that are valued. Most organizations and units hold award ceremonies at which they honor the employees whose behavior best reflects the culture's values. Whether the honor is for the highest sales, the most innovative cost cutting, or the most community volunteer work, it reflects what is important to the culture and illustrates how employees are supposed to behave.

Similarly, the stories that are told about the founders of the organization or unit, their motives, their struggles, the actions that illuminate their character, are selected to illustrate what is important to the culture. Unless it's intended to illustrate how much the organization has changed, you never will hear that

Box 2.2
What Culture Does

An organization's (unit's) culture:

✓ Defines what is of primary importance, the standards against which successes and failures should be measured;

✓ Prescribes how resources are to be used and to what ends;

✓ Establishes what employees can expect from each other;

✓ Makes some methods of controlling behavior legitimate and others illegitimate; that is, it defines where power lies and how it is to be used;

✓ Dictates the behaviors in which employees should or should not engage and specifies how these are to be rewarded and punished;

✓ Sets the tone for how employees should treat each other and how they should treat non-employees: competitively, collaboratively, honestly, distantly, or hostilely; and

✓ Instructs employees about how to deal with the external environment: aggressively, exploitatively, responsibly, or proactively.

In short, the culture prescribes and proscribes; it defines the "dos and don'ts" that govern the behavior of the organization's or unit's employees.

the founder was, in fact, unimaginative, money-grubbing, ruthless, and boorish, because it doesn't serve the cultural need for examples of its values.

Conventions to which employees spontaneously and voluntarily adhere also reflect the culture. For example, an organization that values professionalism and sophistication (e.g., big law firms and financial institutions) will be populated with men in expensive suits and silk ties and women in equally expensive suits and silk blouses. Organizations that value "being genuine and focusing on work" (e.g., those that employ professors, architects, and computer technicians) will be populated with men in shirtsleeves and baggy pants and women in slacks and baggy sweaters. If someone from either of these organizations were to wander into the other one, they would stand out like a sore thumb. If those same people were to come to work in the garb of the people in the other organization, they would be harshly treated by their peers; he who dresses too casually in the first organization will be regarded as unprofessional, warned, and then fired; he who dresses too formally in the second organization will be regarded as pretentious, ridiculed, and sidelined. In short, by dressing like your peers, and by conforming to the other conventions of your organization, you signal that you want to be accepted by the group and that you accept its values.

Beliefs

Beliefs are slightly different from values. They are notions about how things work and what the result will be if you do this or that. For example, suppose that the cultural belief of the retail division of a bank was that customer service is key to everything. Therefore its plan to create demand for financial products (loans, investments, etc.) in the branch banks would honor this belief by striving to provide exceptional service and adapting the products to customer needs in order to create a loyal base of repeat customers. The cultural belief in a different bank's retail division might be that customers come and go and there is nothing that can be done to retain them. Its plan to create demand would reflect this belief by fostering a large turnover in customers so there will always be new people coming into the system with new needs for existing products. In short, the consequence of this difference in beliefs is very different actions; the first bank's plan stresses customer retention and investment in good service and product revision, and the second bank's plan stresses customer recruitment with little investment in service or in product revision. (A third bank may believe in both retention and recruitment and beat the other two, but that's another story.)

To carry this a little further, an organization or unit having a cultural belief that most people are inherently shiftless will treat its employees in a distinctively different way than one that believes that most people have a strong work ethic. An organization or unit that believes that anything is fair as long as you have the power to get away with it probably will treat everyone worse than one that believes that power has proper and improper uses and penalizes improper uses. An organization or unit that believes that the way it does things is the only way to do them probably has already seen its best days and is about to disappear.

You need to understand your organization's and your unit's cultures because they influence your boss's, your own, and your employees' expectations, decisions, and actions. So, if you want to understand why people in your workplace do what they do, it helps to know something about the values and beliefs that motivate them. This is particularly important when your ideas and actions meet with resistance: employees (and managers) resist anything that they interpret as violating expectations deriving from their culture's beliefs and values. Resistance may consist of passively failing to do what is asked of them or of actively refusing to do it—forcing a confrontation that in the view of the resisters is both principled and morally justified. The confrontation will be a complete mystery to you if you don't know the expectations, values, and beliefs that underlie it.

Culture usually reinforces the status quo, and it therefore can be an obstacle to change. Efforts to change the unit, however well intended and necessary, must take the culture into consideration. If the new vision and the plan to achieve it require even minor changes in processes and procedures, those changes will meet resistance if they run counter to expectations based on the culture's values and beliefs. This is awkward because leadership is primarily about change. It can succeed only by taking the culture into account and either working with it or modifying it so the necessary changes no longer violate expectations based on it.

Discovering Your Organization's or Unit's Culture

A culture can be thought of as an organization's or unit's personality. And, just as you can sketch a person's personality using a few adjectives, you can sketch an organization's or unit's culture using a few adjectives; the sketch is just that, a sketch, but it can be useful (see Box 2.3). Research shows that simple inventories, like the one described in the Appendix, can give you a pretty good handle on your organization's or unit's culture. The inventory in the Appendix helps you identify the high points and low points of the culture—what the employees who are enmeshed in that culture think are its most desirable and most undesirable characteristics; these are the people who count because they are either going to accept your proposed changes or reject them, and their decision will turn on how well the changes mesh with their expectations, which are based on the culture as they understand it.

It is unlikely that you can do anything about the organization's culture; you simply have to work around it if you want to introduce change in your unit. But you can strive to modify your unit's culture if it engenders resistance to the changes your unit needs to make to attain its vision.

How to Modify Your Unit's Culture

Let's assume you are planning to introduce some necessary process or procedural changes that you think your employees will find objectionable (i.e., that violate their expectations) because they run counter to the culture. These changes are prescribed by the vision and plan, which at least some of the employees endorse because they helped formulate them. Even at that, they may feel a bit uneasy now that they've had time to think about it, and the other employees may take an immediate dislike to what is being proposed. Presuming you think the changes are crucial enough to justify the effort, you

Box 2.3

Features of the Culture
of a Bank's Retail Division

This list was constructed by a committee of employees that was given the task of identifying the major features of the culture of the Retail Division of a major American bank, which we will call Big Bank. The Appendix contains the cultural inventory based upon this list, together with instructions for scoring the inventory and interpreting its results.

Big Bank's Retail Division Culture

I. Features Centering on Employees

1 = Caring
2 = Learning & Development
3 = Motivation
4 = Communication
5 = Empowerment

II. Features Centering on Customers

 6 = Respect
 7 = Relationships
 8 = Technology
 9 = Team Selling
10 = Expansion

III. Features Centering on the Community

11 = Integrity
12 = Leadership
13 = Responsiveness

must try to modify those parts of the culture that they violate so that they no longer do so.

It does little good to simply tell people that the things they value and believe are counterproductive and that they ought to moderate or completely change them—ideology seldom responds to logic. Indeed, such words are bound to backfire because they are a clear assault on the culture, and that culture provides predictability and legitimacy for what goes on in the unit. Challenging it merely introduces uncertainty about what to expect and about what is and what is not legitimate, and uncertainty tends to cause people to dig in their heels and resist the very cultural modifications you are asking for.

Let's return to our Cataloging Department example. A component of the unit's culture is the belief that competitiveness among the Catalogers and among the Stackers increases productivity, although, in fact, competitiveness is interfering with the unit's productivity rather than enhancing it. Recall that the competitiveness contributes to an uneven workflow from the Catalogers to the Stackers, to which the latter respond by competitively racing to see who can shelve the most books in a day. The result is unacceptable inaccuracy in cataloging and equally unacceptable inaccuracy in shelving. Inaccurate cataloging means the books are classified incorrectly, so readers don't even know the library owns them. Inaccurate shelving means that the books are essentially lost, so researchers may know the books are in the library but nobody can find them. The remedy clearly centers on reducing the competitive racing among Catalogers and Stackers and inducing them both to slow down so they are more accurate, as well as introducing a way of checking on the accuracy of their work. You can bet, however, that merely telling them to slow down and be more careful isn't going to change things much—that urge to compete is still part of the culture and is going to keep popping up again when you aren't looking.

As you can see, culture and expectation modification must be done indirectly, and *behavior changes* are the key. That is, experience shows that culture and expectation modification starts with asking people to change what they do—usually the processes and procedures to which they have become accustomed, but sometimes the ways in which they treat each other or expect to be treated by the organization, if that is what stands in the way of the unit's achieving its vision. If at all possible, the requested behavior changes should be small to begin with, so employees can see that the culture is bent but not broken by the new ways of doing things. As the new behaviors become routine and unthreatening, the culture and expectations will adjust to accommodate them. When things are well established, you then introduce another round of small changes, and so on. Eventually the incremental changes will add up to the major change you wanted in the first place.

Back to the library: to change the Catalogers' dysfunctional competitiveness, your first task is to make sure that you aren't causing the problem by inadvertently setting excessively high expectations for output, expectations that the Catalogers think can only be met by unbridled competition. Presuming you aren't the cause of the Catalogers' competitiveness, you must look for a way to regulate it so it doesn't arouse the Stackers' competitiveness, cascading into problems for the Lending Department. Then you have to find a way to ensure greater accuracy in both cataloging and shelving of the books. To that end, you might set up teams of Catalogers, perhaps one person to cataloge and another one to check for accuracy. Each team might have a target for the day, and rewards in the form of recognition for good performance would depend on how closely each team hit its target. Of course, everyone would have to agree on how to set the targets, but the goal is to adjust them gradually to find the optimum for overall unit performance. Note that this strategy would turn the competitiveness for volume among individual Catalogers into competitiveness among teams for hitting their targets, requiring only a small change in the culture. By reducing volume, you might be able to reduce competition among Stackers, thus increasing shelving accuracy, but you'd have to implement your changes with the Catalogers first so you could see how it affected the Stackers. If the latter still were competing, you might try teams with them too, two persons—one doing the shelving and the other checking for accuracy. However well this all works, it is going to take a while before the teams function smoothly and the Catalogers and Stackers feel comfortable; they've been competing as individuals for a long time and they've valued volume above accuracy. You must give them time to adjust, but you also must be persistent in incrementally moving their behavior and their expectations (hence, the culture) into line with the new plan.

Incremental behavioral change, with its incremental modification of the culture and the expectations that derive from it, is always best, if you have the time. This method of modifying the culture is generally referred to as cultural evolution and is similar to what happens as the culture and expectations adjust to the naturally occurring changes in the unit's environment. But, if behavioral changes and cultural modification must be rapid, you haven't time for cultural evolution, you need cultural revolution—and that means you've got a big problem. Plunging ahead with the full changes that are needed is almost certain to violate the culture and the expectations that derive from it, neither of which will have time to adjust. This is going to arouse resentment and resistance from your employees.

Cultural Evolution

Process and procedural changes that are unaccompanied by culture and expectation change will be temporary—eventually the unit will backslide to where it was before. This means that, if you have the time, the cultural groundwork must be done either beforehand or concurrently with the proposed behavior changes. It also means that the behavior changes must be introduced with the consent and cooperation of the unit's employees—you must never try to trick or manipulate them into making changes of which they disapprove. Usually this involves making them aware of the reasons for changes, the ways in which the changes address those reasons, the cultural compromises that will be required, and how those compromises balance against the good things that can be expected to result from the changes or the bad things that can be avoided—this seldom will change their misgivings about cultural violations, but it can buy you permission to make the first round of small changes to see how they work out. These small changes must be accompanied by an "exit strategy," assurances that if the proposed small changes produce bad results, among which is unacceptable injury to the culture, or do not produce the expected good results, there will be a way to undo them and return to the status quo. That is, "If we start to compromise our values, become too uncomfortable, or do things we suspect may be wrong, or if we don't get the results we hope for, we will reassess the situation and select a more suitable course of action." Along with this assurance, you have to be up front about the fact that things are going to change, that the culture will have to shift to accommodate those changes, that expectations are going to go unmet during the process (and will eventually have to change), or the unit cannot achieve the goals that comprise its vision. Perhaps the employees will decide that the price is too high and that they prefer a scaled-down vision with less ambitious goals. If that happens, you have to decide if you can live with it or if it is time for you to look for your own exit strategy.

In summary, there are three rules for helping a unit's culture evolve:

- Ask only for incremental changes in procedures and processes.
- Let each increment become routine and sink into the culture and expectations before going on to the next increment.
- Be up front about what you are doing—each increment is an experiment that can be reversed if it seems wrong or doesn't work.

Once your employees have agreed to make the incremental changes in their behavior, you can track the culture's evolution (and hasten it to some degree) by seeing how willing they are to instruct others in how to do it, for example, or be a spokesperson for the unit about the efficacy of the changes. Resistance to being publicly associated with the changes means that the culture and expectations haven't evolved enough yet, but as that resistance declines, you know the time is coming for another round of incremental change.

Cultural Revolution

Although evolution usually is the best way to change a culture, there are times when revolution is necessary. Units that have become ossified, that have lost the ability to adapt to changes in their operating environment, sometimes are so resistant to evolution that when life-threatening crises arise, nothing short of revolution will save them (see Box 2.4).

Revolution differs from evolution primarily in terms of its abruptness and magnitude. Revolution allows less for participation by the employees in formulating the changes, and it is less indulgent of the need for assurance about exit strategies if the behavior changes do not work out as expected. It generally is motivated by a sense of urgency that argues for doing something now, doing something big, and doing something permanent! And, unless it is tempered with a good deal of good sense, it is bound to arouse resentment and resistance.

The success of attempts to instigate cultural revolution depends on how severely the required behavior changes violate the existing culture and its expectations. At one extreme, employees will go along with the manager's proposed behavior changes if these changes do not violate the unit's existing culture and their own expectations very much. If the degree of violation is too small to alarm them, employees lack a solid reason for rejecting the changes, although they may not be completely comfortable. At the other extreme, if employees are fully convinced that the status quo is doomed and the unit will suffer if something is not done, they may go along with the proposed changes, even if they severely violate the culture and their expectations, simply because neither will matter much anyway if something dire happens to the unit. There are, of course, degrees in between these two extremes, usually resulting in more or fewer employees willing to accept the changes, all with more or less conviction that it is the right thing to do.

Minor Violations. Consider the case in which the proposed new processes and procedures, while revolutionarily different from what is currently being done, are only minor violations of the culture and employees' resultant expectations. Here your task is to persuade employees that these minor violations should be tolerated because failure to make the changes ensures that the foreseeable, gloomy, future will violate the culture and their expectations even worse. Of course, there will be debates in the hallways and at the water cooler about whether these particular changes are the best ones or whether the threat could not be met just as well with even smaller changes that are not so stressful, but things usually can be worked out because nobody is adamantly resisting the change on principle.

Major Violations. In contrast, even when employees can be convinced that the foreseeable future is incompatible with the culture and their expectations, proposed changes that are major violations of them are likely to meet with

Box 2.4

Changing a Culture Is Like Falling in Love

Indulge me while I draw what I hope will be an instructive, if somewhat strained, analogy between changing a culture and falling in love.

Romance novels teach us that there are two ways to fall in love. The "Old Fashioned Way" is to find someone suitable, marry them, and grow to love them as you work together to build a satisfying life. The "Modern Way" is to fall passionately in love and, if it is "the real thing," depend on the passion lasting a lifetime.

The first way is reasoned, patient, and a little dull—few songs are written about it (what rhymes with diaper?). It is expected that affection, and then love, will develop slowly over a long courtship and become stronger throughout many years of marriage—passion is nice, but not required. The second way is intoxicating, impatient, and irrepressible—most songs are about it (and diapers are never mentioned). Lovers experience a transformative rush of passion, so strong that it surely must endure. But, it is unrealistic to expect such strong emotions to last—they don't mix well with the mundane duties of everyday life. If the lovers can stick it out through the cooling phase, change their expectations, and work together, they often can build a very satisfying life (perhaps with a little passion from time to time). If they can't change their expectations, they usually return to the single life and try again.

Now for the analogy: Consider the parallel between evolutionary culture change and the Old Fashioned Way of falling in love. Evolutionary change is reasoned, patient, and a little dull—passion is nice, but not required. By agreeing to incremental changes in what they do, and patiently, if not enthusiastically, enduring the transient discomforts brought on by those changes, employees will move the unit toward its vision. In the process, the culture and the expectations deriving from it will evolve to accommodate the new ways of doing things and eventually everyone will be better off and, presumably, happier. Now consider the parallel between revolutionary culture change and the Modern Way of falling in love. For the leaders of the revolution at any rate, revolution often is accompanied by a sense of urgency that approaches passion: intoxicating, impatient, and irrepressible. It demands transformative changes quickly. If employees can be convinced to join the revolution—if they are willing to endure the discomfort and persevere—the revolution can achieve the same result that evolution would have yielded: a reformed culture, survival, and prosperity. If they decline to join the revolution or if they find the discomfort too much to endure, they will return to the status quo, perhaps to try again.

resistance: confrontations, arguments, insubordination, discontented gossip, slowed productivity, increased turnover, reduced coordination of activities, and a general sense of dissatisfaction.

In the face of resistance, you have three avenues for getting the changes the unit must have:

- You can get tough, unilaterally impose changes, and then pick up the pieces afterward.
- You can try to convince employees that the crisis facing the unit is so large that it justifies changes, however distasteful they may be.
- If you somehow can buy time, you can try to tone down the revolution to something like a speeded-up evolution, making iterations of small changes in the hope that things will change before time runs out.

If the crisis facing the unit is acute and there is little time to spare, unilaterally imposing changes may be the only avenue open to you. If other jobs are open to them, employees may leave. Often those who leave are the people who most strongly identify with the existing culture. Their skills may be missed, but, on the other hand, you can fill their positions with new people who have no stake in the current culture. If leaving is not practical, disgruntled employees may decide to fight the changes, and the ensuing strife can badly weaken both you and the unit—and you may lose the battle. Even if you win, your employees are not going to forget that you rolled right over them—nobody likes being bullied. This is a very risky way to introduce change.

The second avenue, convincing employees that the crisis is so pressing that violations of the culture and expectations are acceptable, is better, but it too has its downside. On the one hand, in order to convince them, you usually have to frame your arguments in terms of present or potential threats to what is important to them—which is the existing culture and the continued existence of their jobs. On the other hand, that very culture is violated by the proposed changes, which may make their jobs less attractive. It is not unlike the famous quotation from the Vietnam War, "In order to save the village, we had to destroy it."

The third avenue for instigating change in an organization, through small changes in activities that change the culture and expectations so that large changes become acceptable, converts the revolution into a rushed evolution. If you go too fast, you may quickly reach a point at which employees resist any further increments. This can leave things stranded in mid course; the old culture is in flux because of the rush of incremental changes, but has not yet evolved to the point that it can embrace the full extent of change that is needed to put the unit on track toward its goals. This is the time for leadership, urging employees to endure their discomfort and distress in order to get the job of changing done so that there is a reasonable chance of success. You may have to use a little of each of the previous two avenues to do this, but this will be the test of your ability to manage your unit. You won't be very popular, but there is time for that later; success tends to heal everyone's wounds.

Ethics

Attempting to change a unit's culture is very serious business. You are, after all, tinkering with peoples' values and beliefs in order to achieve a rather material end—the success of your unit. Your employees, as well as the organization, will be affected by what you do, so it behooves you to give it a good deal of thought before you do anything. No doubt you'll tell yourself that you are only going to change the culture a little, just enough to accommodate what must be done to move the unit along. But, you may be kidding yourself; after all, the current culture may be quite adequate for what must be done and what you have in mind might degrade it, rather than improve it. You don't want to cause unnecessary damage simply to demonstrate your managerial abilities and further your career—right?

We will talk more about ethics in Chapter 5, but for the moment, let me give you an example of a destructive change in the ethical component of a unit's culture. I had an acquaintance, who, upon becoming the head of a department, immediately set about changing the culture for the worse. I'm sure this wasn't his intention, but it is what happened. When he took over, the unit was doing reasonably well, but considerably below its potential. He soon had achieved such success that the unit was frequently featured in the organization's quarterly magazine and in the local newspaper—always with a picture of him.

Unfortunately, to achieve this success, my acquaintance had convinced his employees that corners had to be quietly cut, records subtly falsified, and deals made under the table. His assistant (who was something of a thug to begin with) was more than willing to help him and to convince others that it was okay because it, supposedly, was the only way for the unit to succeed. As these questionable practices became accepted, the culture and expectations about how one ought to behave changed accordingly, largely because they appeared to work. And, as is so often the case, at the zenith of the unit's apparent success, my acquaintance left for a more exalted job elsewhere.

The woman who took over after he left discovered the irregularities he left behind and, after looking into them, publicly revealed every detail. As a result, the unit's star fell considerably faster than it had risen, and its tarnished reputation persisted long after its faults had been corrected. Tragically, some of the employees found that shortcuts and shady practices were hard habits to break. After repeated warnings, there were dismissals and new people were hired in an attempt to eradicate the flawed culture the former manager had built. Ironically, he had undermined a respectable, if lackluster culture to establish an unquestionably bad culture in the name of helping the unit, and that bad culture damaged the unit almost beyond repair. With each new set of revelations, we who were bystanders were shocked and, belatedly, outraged. (The people at the manager's new job clearly were smarter than we were; they quickly figured out what he was up to and he left, never to be heard of again.)

My acquaintance didn't seem to me to be a bad man, and I don't think he was generally unethical. It is just that his ethics didn't seem to extend to his career; he wanted success so much that anything that would bring it was good, by definition. I doubt that it ever occurred to him that there were ethical issues involved at all—he wasn't proposing to murder anyone or steal anything, he was just controlling the way things looked to outsiders so that his unit appeared in the very best light. I'll bet he still attributes the unit's decline after he left to the inability of his successors to do the job as well as he did.

Ethics is a major issue in any enterprise because ethical lapses, while costly, are so common. Therefore, we'll pick up this discussion again in future chapters.

Summary

To ensure mastery of the material in this chapter, summarize it for yourself by filling in this topic outline.

I. Managerial Units _____

_____

A. Definition _____

_____

B. The Maintenance/Change Decision _____

_____

C. The Unit as a Mini-Enterprise _____

_____

D. The Leader's Job _____

_____

E. Collaboration _____

_____

II. Culture   _____

_____

A. Values _____

_____

B. Beliefs _____

_____

C. Discovering Your Organization's or Unit's Culture _____

_____

D. How to Modify Your Unit's Culture _____

_____

1. Cultural Evolution _____

_____

2. Cultural Revolution _____

_____

i. Minor Violations _____

_____

ii. Major Violations _____

_____

III. Ethics   _____

_____

Exercises

1. Arrange to interview three people who currently manage one or more employees. One person should be a small-business owner, a second should be in a nonprofit organization, and the third should be in a medium to large for-profit organization. Prior to each interview, write each question on the top of a clean sheet of paper and write your notes about the person's answer on the sheet below the question. Questions

should focus on the topics discussed in this chapter. At the close of the interview, ask permission to return with further questions. Future interviews will focus on the topics of each of the chapters following this one. (If you do not know suitable managers, ask your instructor for suggestions and a letter or phone call introducing you to the person.)

2. Write a short essay on the results of your interviews, comparing the answers given by the three managers. Attempt to integrate what you have learned from the text and from your interviews into a personal viewpoint about managing employees.

3. Place this and future essays in a notebook to create a record of your views about managing employees.

Sources and Further Reading

Beach, L.R. (1993). *Making the right decision: Organizational culture, vision, and planning.* Englewood Cliffs, NJ: Prentice Hall.

Beach, L.R. (2005). *Leadership and the art of change.* Thousand Oaks, CA: Sage.

Bernick, C.L. (2001). When your culture needs a makeover. *Harvard Business Review, 79,* 53–59.

Beyer, J.M. (1981). Ideologies, values, and decision making in organizations. In P. C. Nystrom & W. H. Starbuck (Eds.), *Handbook of organizational design.* New York: Oxford.

Denhardt, R.B., & Denhardt, J.V. (2006). *The dance of leadership: The art of leading in business, government, and society.* Armonk, NY: Sharpe.

Harrison, R. (1972, May–June). Understanding your organization's character. *Harvard Business Review, 81,* 41–46.

Sathe, V. (1983, Autumn). Implications of corporate culture: A manager's guide to action. *Organizational Dynamics,* 5–23.

3

Understanding Expectations

*Good managers commit to understanding their own and their
employees' work-related expectations and how they affect behavior.*

In the preceding chapter (Chapter 2), we discussed the beliefs and values that
constitute an organization or unit's culture, and how they shape the expectations of members of the organization about how they and the other members
should be treated and how they should behave. In this chapter, we will expand
on the concept of expectations and their role in guiding workplace behavior,
and examine some of the implications for you as a manager.

What Expectations Do

Each of us has many beliefs and values, only a subset of which is related to the
workplace. There are other subsets: for your family, for example, or for your
religious faith, and so on. All of these subsets influence your expectations, but
the subset that pertains to a particular setting (work; home; church, temple,
or mosque) has precedence when you are in that setting. There is, of course,
some spillover from one setting to another—for example, most people's religious beliefs and values exert an influence across different settings, not just
their place of worship—but the subset that is specific to a particular setting
usually has the greatest influence.

Expectations and Scenarios

Expectations derive from beliefs and values and are mentally encoded as
story-like vignettes you tell yourself—rather like sketchy little plays you act

out in your head—the technical name for which is *scenarios*. Scenarios are seldom worked out in much detail—they usually are simple and bear on a single theme. They consist of both verbal narrative (the little voice in your head) and visual fragments (your "mind's eye"), all of which meld into a rough description of what should happen in a particular setting, given your beliefs and values related to that setting. The operative phrase in that last sentence is *what should happen,* because the scenario tells you what to expect your own behavior, or the behavior of others, to look like if it conforms to the demands of your beliefs and values. That is, expectations are standards against which we judge our own and others' actual behavior.

- If there is little or no discrepancy between your expectations and what you or others in fact do, you simply move on. After all, that is what you expected.
- If there is a favorable discrepancy, you are pleased. For example, if you try something and exceed your expectations or if someone is nicer than you expected, you are pleasantly surprised.
- If there is an unfavorable discrepancy, that is, your expectations have been "*violated,*" you are displeased. For example, if your performance falls short of your expectations or if someone is unexpectedly rude, you are unpleasantly surprised and you may try to do something to eliminate the unfavorable discrepancy—you could practice the faulty skill or try to find out why the person was rude.

Threats

There are two kinds of expectations; expectations about what ideally *should* happen and expectations about what actually *might* happen. "Should" is a requirement; "might" is a prediction. When there is a discrepancy between "should" expectations and "might" expectations, alarms go off in your head warning you that things don't appear to be going well.

Although the word "expectation" implies anticipation of future events, in a sense expectations work both backward and forward in time. That is, after something has already happened, you can compare it with your "should" expectations by generating a scenario about how it ought to have happened—if reality and the scenario match, fine. If reality exceeds or falls short of your "should" expectations, you experience happiness or unhappiness, respectively, about what happened, with efforts to prolong the happiness or to stop the unhappiness.

Similarly, you can anticipate future events by generating a scenario about what might happen in the situation and compare it with your "should" expectations. If it looks like they will match, fine. If it looks like the "might" will exceed your "should" expectations, you experience guarded optimism. But, if it looks like your "should" expectations will be violated by anticipated events, you experience anxious pessimism. Anticipated events that arouse anxious pessimism are called *threats,* and threats motivate you to do something to prevent the threatening events from happening—to keep your "might" expectations from being realized. If you can't prevent the threatening event from happening, you usually try to escape from the situation before it does.

Beliefs and Values

Your work-related beliefs and values are partly your own and partly the result of accepting the organization's and unit's cultures. Your beliefs and values for other areas of your life derive from your life experience, starting from your childhood and growing throughout your lifetime.

Beliefs

Beliefs are rules acquired through experience, instruction, or rational thought. They tell you what should happen as a result of something else happening. If the sun shines, it will get warmer outside; if you're nice to people, they'll be nice to you; if you pray for a person who is ill, they will get better; if you work hard, you will succeed; if you exercise and eat right, you will be healthier. In short, beliefs are cause-and-effect rules of the form, If X —> then Y. "If X happens, it will cause Y to happen," or "If I make X happen, then Y will happen."

Because they are rules, beliefs create expectations: you expect X to produce Y. Of course, you know that there are exceptions to every rule, but you nonetheless react with surprise, distress, and disappointment when your rule fails and Y doesn't follow X. And you experience anxiety when there is a threat that the rule will fail and your expectation won't be met. (Even if the rule works, you aren't always happy—too much Y can sometimes be as bad as too little, but that's another story.)

The negative emotions aroused by the actual or threatened violation of your expectations leads you to:

- Attempt to leave the situation;
- Attempt to make sure failure doesn't happen if it hasn't happened yet;
- Attempt to make sure failure doesn't happen again if it already has happened.

Values

Values are standards of merit. They tell you what is worthy of desire and what isn't, what is moral or ethical and what isn't, what is appropriate and what isn't, what people should do and what they shouldn't: greed is bad; courtesy is good; loafing is bad; hard work is good; keeping busy is good; striving for self-improvement is good; cheating, stealing, and lying are all bad, and so on. Like beliefs, values are acquired through experience, instruction, and rational thought, with the foundations laid down in early childhood. The result is a mixture of important standards, called morals and ethics, and less important standards for things like table manners and social etiquette.

Values create expectations about what people should respect or cherish, and about how they, and you, should behave. When you or others fall short of these expectations, you experience negative emotions that range anywhere from peevishness to outrage, depending on the severity of the violation and the importance of the value. This emotion usually is coupled with a desire to punish or reform the offender (you or someone else) to make sure the violation does not recur. If you value music, the person who devalues it by talking during a concert arouses your ire and may prompt you to tell them to hush—although social conventions, which you also value, usually limit you to dirty looks. If you value courtesy and someone in a waiting room insists on holding a loud cell phone conversation, you become irritated and want them to stop—although social convention again limits your reactions.

As with threats to belief-based expectations, threats to value-based expectations arouse anxiety and lead to attempts to leave the situation or to do something to make sure the threat doesn't materialize.

Beliefs and values are not independent of one another. The reason you're upset when X doesn't lead to Y is because Y is something you value—as you might have guessed, values give value to things. For example, if the organization's cultural beliefs and your own private beliefs both hold that hard work will be rewarded, you are likely to assume that if you work hard, the organization will reward you with something you value. Your expectation will be pretty strong; after all, you value the reward and there are two sets of beliefs, the culture's and your own, that lead you to believe the "work —> reward" rule will work. However, if you begin to suspect that the rule isn't going to work (a threat), you will become anxious, which might prompt you to seek assurance from your boss, or perhaps you might begin to look for a job where the rule is more clearly going to work. If you don't suspect the rule won't work, that is, you don't sense a threat, but then you find out that your hard work will go unrewarded, your reaction will reflect both the belief violation (disappointment) and the value violation (outrage).

That is a pretty heavy mix of emotions, so it should not be surprising if it leads to equally heavy behavior.

Violations

As we've said, expectations are violated when there is an undesirable discrepancy between what is expected and what actually happens, or, in the case of threat, between what is expected and what might happen. Beyond some small comfort zone, the greater the discrepancy the greater your reaction will be. That is, small violations may be ignored because they don't exceed your comfort zone; for all intents and purposes they count as though your expectations had been met. Just beyond your comfort zone, violations trigger a little emotion, but only enough to motivate you to take moderate and reasoned action to prevent a threatening event or repair an existing violation and prevent its recurrence. Large violations trigger large emotions and prompt large efforts to head off the threat or straighten things out if they've already gone awry.

"Hot Buttons"

The strength of your reaction to threats or to actual violations of particular expectations may sometimes surprise even you. These "hot buttons" have very small comfort zones, and your strong reaction can lead you to do things you'll later regret—anything from complaining, to being rude, to starting to cry, to having a temper tantrum, to becoming violent. Moreover, hot buttons leave you open to manipulation by other people who intentionally "push your buttons" to get predictable responses. Therefore, it is a good idea to know your own hot buttons and to come up with ways of heading off an overreaction when they get pushed. Similarly, it's a good idea to identify your employees' hot buttons so you can understand why they react the way they do.

Short of psychoanalysis, I know of no well-formulated way of identifying hot buttons—and psychoanalysis probably would focus on why they're hot in the first place, which may be more than you want to know. A more rough-and-ready method is to keep track of incidents that suggest that you or your employees have had your buttons pushed. Review of these incidents can provide enough insight for your purposes. Although the "Mother of All Hot Buttons" may be lurking somewhere waiting to be pushed, you can't worry about it, because you need practical information for dealing with day-to-day events, not the mega-meltdowns (although we'll discuss mega-meltdowns—sometimes called "going postal"—in Chapter 4).

A clue about hot buttons is provided by identifying the topics and events that everybody steers clear of when they're around you or around one of your employees. Knowing a person well includes knowing what not to say or do around them if you don't want to set them off on a diatribe or make them so uncomfortable they become angry or leave. That means that friends can be a source of information about hot buttons, but you have to be careful how you ask—they will be reluctant to tell you about yourself, and you don't want it to look like you're spying on your employees. This is dangerous territory for everyone simply because hot buttons are hot for a reason—the associated beliefs and values are important.

Try this little exercise: Think of four people you have worked with at one time or other and write the letters A through D on a sheet of paper. Then consider each person for a moment and jot down the things you know you couldn't discuss with him or her because you would get a passionate lecture, simply hit a wall, or make them angry—sex and other personal issues probably don't count. Do this for each person and then do it at the bottom of the page for yourself, as if you were someone else thinking about you and what upsets you. At first you'll only have one big thing for each person, but a little more thinking probably will bring up a couple more—and that's really all you need to get the general idea. Then try to imagine what expectations you would be violating if you were to venture to discuss the forbidden topic with them.

I realize this exercise is sort of cheap and unreliable psycho-something, but if you don't take it too seriously, it can be informative—or at least it can suggest some interesting questions. When I did it, I came up with: Person A's big hot button is authority; he has rebelled against every boss he's ever had, bad-mouthing them to anyone who would listen—to the detriment of his career. The only time I tried to talk with him about it as a friend, he, in effect, left the scene; his eyes glazed over and he promptly changed the subject. Person B's hot button is lack of control, especially at work; she can get mean when things don't run exactly the way she wants them to. To my knowledge, nobody has ever had the courage to talk with her about it. Person C's button is lack of structure; when things get messy, she gets anxious and angry. She knows this about herself but is powerless to do anything, so she wisely goes out of her way to avoid unstructured situations. Person D's is boundaries; constraints on his creativity, even when justified, upset him and lead to arguments or his abrupt departure. Finally, my own hot button is criticism; I do not take it well—or even a little bit well. My wife tried to help me, but she gave up—good thing too, because I hate being criticized for reacting badly to criticism. (Box 3.1 contains a little more about Persons A through D.)

The primary value of identifying your own and others' hot buttons is that you can think about how to avoid or defuse them ahead of time. For example, I know I should learn to take criticism well, but I also know I'm never going

Box 3.1

Hot Buttons

From what I have learned in conversations with him, Person A's father was exceedingly authoritarian, ruling his family with an iron hand and belittling his children as a form of punishment. Tired of clashing with his father, Person A left home as soon as he could, worked his way through school, and became quite good at what he does. However, he still reacts emotionally to people in authority and behaves toward them much as he behaved toward his father—resentfully, rudely, and rebelliously. Those on the receiving end of this behavior are, of course, shocked and angered (he violates their expectations), with the result that rewards for his very good job performance come much harder than they do for other people. In his eyes, of course, this lack of reward confirms that anyone in authority is bound to undervalue him and his work—which keeps the cycle going.

Person B grew up in a small town at a time when women were supposed to excel, but demurely. She did very well in school and is quite bright and very able. Unfortunately, her career has advanced to the point that the demands of her high-powered job push the limits of her abilities; she constantly feels vulnerable and on the edge of being overwhelmed. Her insecurity leads her to be more controlling than she might otherwise be. Those who work for her either love her or hate her; the former being people who don't mind being micromanaged and the rest being people who loath it. Of course, she can't actually control everything, and the stress from trying to do so is taking a toll on her health. As a result, she is considering retirement, although the idea of not being in charge of something distresses her.

Person C also is a bright, able woman. She was raised in a very structured environment by Depression-era parents who valued security above everything. As a result, she finds lack of structure very stressful, and her career choices reflect it. Most of her jobs have allowed her to structure things the way she wants them and to function almost exclusively within that structure. Whenever she finds herself in unstructured situations, she reacts with such acute anxiety she has to find a quick way out. On the bright side, her employers always are pleased by her ability to organize things and make them operate smoothly.

I don't know much about Person D's background. I only know that he is bright and creative, and that he hates to operate within prescribed boundaries. The causal observer might think he was rebelling against authority, but in fact he is just fine with authority until it tries to restrain his extravagant plans. He likes to design production programs, but they often end up crossing the line between his unit's resources and other units' resources, and they usually are so different from the organization's other programs that they arouse mistrust. Attempts to explain that his creative ideas sometimes make more problems than they solve are interpreted by him as the whining of timid people who are afraid of innovation, a topic upon which he expands at the least provocation. Perhaps he is correct in thinking that the innovations he wants would be good, but he seldom has the opportunity to find out because he alienates everybody whose help he needs to get them accepted.

to. It's far more effective to invest in devising strategies for coping with my reactions to criticism than in trying to reform myself. So, for example, if I receive a letter from an editor criticizing an article or something else that I've written, my strategy is to withdraw to my office, cuss and fuss in private, put the offending letter on the back of my desk until I've cooled down, and then reply civilly and constructively. When someone criticizes me to my face, my strategy is to smile as graciously as I can (which, I am told, isn't all that graciously), vaguely acknowledge the possibility (extremely remote) that the criticism is warranted, withdraw to my office, cuss and fuss, etc. In this regard, I recommend the old adage, "Don't ever let them see you sweat." Learn to control the immediate reaction and work out your feelings later, in private or with someone who is sympathetic, patient, and may be able to help you put things in perspective. The goal isn't to get rid of the hot button, which might take years of therapy; it is to stifle the reaction until you're someplace where it can be released safely.

Expectations in the Workplace

Just as in the other spheres of life, work-life revolves around expectations and what to do when they are unmet or might be unmet. Your employees all have expectations in regard to their jobs. Expectations came with them when they took the job; some were acquired as they learned the organization's and unit's cultures, and some were formed as a result of what you and higher management did and said. Some expectations were strong from the beginning because they derived from the employee's private beliefs and values; the expectation that the job will be rewarding, that there will be opportunities for advancement, that they will be treated well, and so on. Others were acquired through experience on the job. Whether expectations are old or new, their violation is met with disappointment and the threat of a violation is met with anxiety.

Disappointment or anxiety usually leads employees to appeal to someone who has the power to undo the violation or prevent the threat—often that's you. If this doesn't work, the employee has a choice; he or she can look for another job or can try to adjust to the violation (or the threat) in hope that by doing so things will somehow get better without his or her having to quit. If adjustment is the choice, the next step is to tentatively revise the violated expectation to accommodate the event that violated it, or that threatens to violate it. If the tentatively revised expectation isn't jarringly incongruent with his or her underlying beliefs and values, the disappointment or anxiety will dissipate, and the tentative revision becomes permanent—the employee has adjusted. However, if the tentative revision can't be reconciled with the underlying beliefs and values, the employee cannot adjust and must leave.

Dealing with Violations

Grievance

Most employees' first reaction to violated expectations is to complain to family, friends, and coworkers. Upon receiving sympathy and encouragement, they may then take the complaint to their boss (you), seeking redress based on the rightness of their expectations and the wrongness of whatever violated them. Sometimes this works; if you are convinced that the violation was unjust or in error, restitution can be made and things can go back to normal. When it doesn't work, however, disappointment may turn into anger and anger turn into a willingness to fight using the organization's formal grievance process, filing complaints with an outside watchdog agency, or resorting to legal action.

Leaving

When grievance fails, disappointed employees may simply leave. There are two ways of doing this: leaving mentally or leaving physically.

We all know disappointed people who have elected to leave mentally, refusing to change their expectations but refusing to quit their jobs. Stuck in a strange twilight world, they become outdated, occupying a job-slot but often contributing little to the unit's progress. When possible, organizations shed these disengaged people, but sometimes they can't, so they sidetrack them and wait for them to grow weary enough to quit or old enough to retire.

Those who are disappointed but can't adjust usually elect to leave physically. They either transfer elsewhere in the organization, if a more compatible place can be found, or they look for a job in a more congenial organization. This, of course, presumes they can get another job. If the job market is weak, or if they wear their discontent on their sleeve, they may not receive offers. When this happens, they have to choose: alter their expectations, battle the organization, or leave mentally—all possible formulas for chronic discontent.

Revision of Violated Expectations

If grievance doesn't produce redress and leaving isn't attractive, the disappointed employee must adjust. Adjustment requires changing his or her expectations so they are more "realistic" in light of the reason they were violated. For example, if a new employee expects to be treated with courtesy when he takes a job in an organization having a culture that fosters rudeness, he can complain, leave, or get used to it. Getting used to it means that he comes to expect rudeness and no longer takes offense. This revision of his expectation may only extend to the workplace—he still expects people in other settings to be courteous—but adjusting to workplace norms will reduce his discomfort and allow him to stay on the job.

Revision frequently requires a good deal of strength and forbearance; the employee has to bite the bullet and stick with it until he or she sees how things work out. This is almost always stressful because while it is happening his or her expectations are being violated, at first anyway. Nobody is truly happy when they are in the process of revising their expectations; after all, revision begins with accepting an assault on one's beliefs and values and then changing them so the expectations that derive from them are in line with "reality." Beliefs and values are supposed to be bedrock, the things that make the world predictable, the essence of what is right and what is wrong. Bedrock is bedrock because it is stable, so changing it is bound to be difficult. (Note that the process that allows an individual employee to change his or her beliefs, values, and expectations is the same one that underlies culture change at the collective level. No surprise then that culture change meets resistance and causes anguish.)

If sticking it out yields satisfying results, growth occurs, expectations are revised, and beliefs and values change. If sticking it out yields unsatisfying results, there usually is regression to the original beliefs, values, and expectations. For example, let's say that a woman who works for you has been selected to attend a training course that will help her with the technical aspects of her job. Taking time out for the class is likely to compromise her job performance because it will cause her to get behind in her work and require long hours to catch up. She has always believed that training courses were generally useless and that by taking time away from work they do more bad than good. She is particularly threatened by the prospect of her next performance review, which makes her anxious and stressed. But you urge her to take the offered course, and, against her better judgment, she agrees to do it.

Suppose it turns out that everything was just as awful as she expected, and all she has to show for it is a pretty certificate proclaiming her to be trained and a few weeks of long hours catching up on her work. The whole experience only strengthens her negative opinion of training courses. Then she receives an offer of a promotion and raise, based on the fact that she has the necessary training for the offered job. She accepts. Later, over a beer with friends, she thinks aloud about the whole episode and comes to the conclusion that training programs may be worth the hassle; perhaps the only way to grow is to endure discomfort while experimenting with change, and growth opens new doors. (That grinding sound you hear is her beliefs and values shifting.)

Dealing with Threats

Threat of having expectations violated motivates employees to try to prevent the violation or to escape it. They can prevent it either by stopping the threatening event from occurring, by leaving so it can't harm them, or by revising their expectations so they don't get violated after all.

Prevention

When a threat looms, employees frequently seek protection from someone with the power to prevent it—you, your boss, Human Resources, or an influential friend elsewhere in the organization. For example, if they think they might get a less-than-sterling performance review (a threat) because of something that was not their fault, they could come to you with their side of things before the reviews are done. If you buy their story, you rid them of the threat. If not, they might try your boss, Human Resources, or their powerful friend. If this is to no avail, they have to decide whether to leave or to revise their expectations so lower evaluation results are less disappointing.

Leaving

In a sense, leaving is just another form of prevention—if you aren't there, the violation can't occur, or at least it can't hurt you. As before, leaving can be mental or physical. Leaving mentally to avoid a threat is called "denial," and isn't generally regarded as healthy. It simply is a refusal to acknowledge, either to yourself or others, that the threat exists—for example, the employee who buys a house on the dicey conviction that he won't be part of the next round of layoffs.

Leaving physically means taking a job elsewhere, often after appraising the threat and deciding that it is bound to materialize no matter what you do.

Some employees find the simple existence of the threat so distressing that they get out as soon as they can.

Revision of Threatened Expectations

When you or your boss can't protect an employee from a threat and leaving isn't attractive, he or she has to adjust, just as would be the case if the violation had already taken place. Indeed, the mechanism for adjustment is the same; employees must endure the discomfort of threatened expectations as they try to convince themselves that the reality won't be as bad as they think. If this turns out to be true, they can afford to modify their future expectations. If it doesn't turn out to be true, they endure all the pain they anticipated and have to leave.

Implications

Abstract as all of the foregoing may seem, it has some very practical implications for you, as a manager. Indeed, the key to being a successful manager is learning to look at your own and your employees' behavior in light of expectations, threats, violations, and reactions: first, because it helps you understand why you and they do some of the things you do, and second, because it helps you understand how to get them to buy into your efforts to enhance their job performance and the unit's overall performance.

You need to understand why your employees do what they do, why they react as they do, so you can help them when they do the wrong thing. If you can't see what motivates their behavior, that behavior will look arbitrary, or worse, malicious. The fact is, of course, most behavior is simply an attempt to deal with perceived threats and actual violations of expectations, even if nobody else senses the threat or recognizes the violation. Of course, some behavior actually may be arbitrary or malicious, but that doesn't mean it isn't serving a purpose. That purpose is almost always to ward off threats or mitigate violations as people go about the business of living with their expectations. Knowing this, you can look for the underlying expectations and either work around them as you deal with the employee or work on changing them when they create barriers to the employee's success.

You need to understand how threats and violations influence your employees' actions if you are going to motivate them. Requests that are congruent with or exceed expectations will motivate high performance. Requests that threaten expectations will get only grudging compliance or active resistance. If you don't understand these expectations, requests that may seem perfectly reasonable to you may seem wholly inappropriate, even villainous, to your employees. If you ask them to keep records of travel expenses, you may be shocked at their negative reaction. If nobody has ever asked for such records before, the culture may have evolved a belief in the independence and unquestioned honesty of employees. Thus your request for records is seen as an assault on their self-esteem and on the culture—both of which would lead them to expect you to trust in their honesty. As a result, what you see as a reasonable business practice, they see as a threat. This doesn't mean you have to back down, but it means that you have blundered into a problem that may take more time to fix than it would have if you had known about and worked around their expectations.

The simplest way to understand your employees' expectations is to ask. True, people often are not wholly aware of what they expect until a threat arises, but that doesn't justify not trying. This is part of the wisdom of running things by an advisory group or formulating new initiatives in the context of a representative committee—if their alarm bells go off, you will hear them before you make a mess of things. Forewarned, you can figure out strategies of accomplishing that which must be accomplished without getting everybody upset and resistant.

On a more positive note, if you know about them, you can look for ways of meeting your employees' expectations that will also profit the unit. After all, most expectations are good for the individuals who have them and a lot of them are good for the unit. You shouldn't presume that everything you want to do is going to raise hackles; employees have an interest in their own success and the success of the unit, which includes your success. Their expectations generally will be congruent with those interests. Problems arise when their expectations in some particular area are at cross purposes with their own success or the success of the unit, but this is less often than might be imagined, which is what makes it surprising when it happens.

Presumed Obligations

There is a commonly observed phenomenon involving expectations of which every manager should be aware. It occurs when an expectation has always been met and never been threatened. Because it is consistently reaffirmed, the expectation may become so solid and strongly held that employees come to think that the organization is somehow obliged to meet it; after all, it has always done so in the past. For example, if employees receive raises year after year, they often conclude (emotionally if not logically) that the organization is obligated to grant increases every year. If, for some reason, the organization defaults or threatens to default on this presumed obligation, the strong expectation of regular raises is violated and employees will react accordingly.

Even if they understand intellectually that there is no contractual obligation and even if they understand the reasons for the default, they will almost inevitably react with deep disappointment (or anxiety) coupled with a strong sense of betrayal and anger.

Part of your job, as their manager, is to recognize when your employees' expectations are turning into unjustified presumptions of obligation. This isn't to say that you and the organization don't have obligations to the employees; law books are full of them. But presumed obligations are very difficult to deal with; they're lopsided—the employee knows about them but nobody else does. Therefore, when an issue arises about their violation and the employee angrily reacts to what he or she sees as a betrayal of trust, everyone except the employee is surprised.

When you discover that you have an angry employee to deal with, the tendency is either to assuage their anger by giving them what they expected to receive or to simply shrug off the whole incident because you and the organization have no legal obligations. The first reaction is bad because it creates a dangerous precedent—"Throw a tantrum and you'll win." The second is bad because it leaves the employee disillusioned and angry, which is contagious. Coworkers tend to sympathize with those whom they perceive as having been wronged, and sympathy quickly turns into exaggerated sensitivity to even small violations or threats to their own expectations. It is far better to stop the whole thing before it starts by ensuring that unrealistic and unjustified expectations don't arise in the first place.

Beliefs, Values, and Ethics

Discussions of beliefs and values invariably lead to questions about political, religious, and social ideologies, as well as questions about why the behavior of people who profess to believe in those ideologies is so frequently at variance with them.

People misbehave for four reasons:

- They genuinely don't know the right thing to do.
- They know the right thing to do, but they don't know when to do it.
- They know what to do and when, but after the first slip, slipping again gets easier and easier.
- They know what to do and when, but the benefits of misbehaving exceed the costs.

We often do not know the right thing to do. Perhaps we never were taught, or perhaps we were taught but never understood the underlying reasons, so the rules are somewhat arbitrary. When quizzed, few of us actually know much about the ideologies we claim to believe in. In fact, we usually have been taught the practices and prejudices that derive from the ideologies, rather than the substance of the ideologies themselves. That is, we're taught what Democrats or Republicans endorse or condemn but not much more than a few slogans about the political philosophies from which those endorsements or condemnations derive. Similarly, few of us know much about the theological underpinnings of the religion or sect to which we belong. As a result, most of us are pretty sketchy about why the political party we support, the religion we profess, or a social movement we champion requires us to behave in particular ways. Instead, we simply believe, to one degree or other, that the required way is the right way and that the world would be a better place if everyone behaved the way we expect them to. We'll call these rules "behavioral expectations," and they are held with varying degrees of conviction, according to how arbitrary or how immutable we have been taught they are.

Why then do we go astray? Even when we know what to do, why don't we always do it? The answer is that knowing what to do isn't enough if you don't know when to do it. Lacking the philosophical "big picture" that justifies the rules, we have trouble generalizing those rules from one setting to another. As a result, we frequently fail to recognize that our behavioral expectations apply to the situation at hand. These "dangerous situations" in which we so often go astray are dangerous precisely because they are difficult to recognize. Indeed, political analyses, and religious sermons, are attempts to help us identify such situations so we can do the right thing—that is, behave as we "ought to."

But, even with good advice, it's impossible to always know what's right and wrong in dangerous situations, and we all fall short of our own ideals, even if we don't recognize it at the time. Later, when we come to realize that our behavior violated our beliefs about how we ought to behave, we experience guilt—which is a form of anger directed toward oneself. When other people's behavior violates our beliefs about how people ought to behave, we experience anger directed toward them.

My morning newspaper contained the sad story of the president of a college student organization who was issued a credit card to use for the organization's expenses. He claimed that he inadvertently handed the clerk the wrong card when purchasing some camping equipment. He discovered his mistake but instead of correcting it, he went on a spending spree, eventually charging $18,000 worth of sports equipment and a laptop computer. The organization's treasurer contacted the police when he received the credit card statement, and the president was arrested and charged with theft. His defense was that after the first, inadvertent, charge, things just "snowballed." He knew what he was doing was wrong, and he destroyed the card in an effort to stop doing it, but by then it was too late.

This unfortunate example is not uncommon; it is simply another version of people going on eating binges after particularly seductive donuts break their diets, or having a series of extramarital affairs after they get away with the first one. Having violated the rules, it becomes easier to continue doing so even though you know what you're doing is wrong. It's tragic to watch people suffer guilt and shame while continuing to do the very things that produce that guilt and shame—until someone or something stops them. The usual justification is that after the first slip, the thing just snowballed and self-control evaporated.

Finally, of course, there are situations in which we know what to do, but the real or anticipated rewards of breaking the rules are so desirable that they all but obliterate guilt and shame—donuts and affairs sometimes fall in this category, at least the first few do. There may be residual guilt and shame, but they are regarded as a small price, just a nuisance compared to the pleasure obtained by the desired rewards. Often, a binge's initial slip (the discovery that you've misused someone else's credit card or a forbidden pastry) occurs when the attractive rewards for bad behavior overbalance the less attractive rewards of following the rules; the inevitable guilt and shame get lost in the shuffle. Having made this first slip, it is easier to continue slipping.

Unethical Behavior

When behavioral expectations become imperatives, we call them ethics. However, for all their special status as imperatives, the problem of knowing when ethics apply is no different from any other set of expectations about behavior. The result is the same too, an all too common blindness to the ethical flaws in what one is doing and what one is urging others to do. In situations defined by intense competition, the fine line between shrewd behavior and unethical behavior is often hard to discern, and even people who are ethical paragons in other areas of their lives can have difficulties.

As with less noble behavioral expectations, the primary problem with ethics seldom is that one doesn't have them, it's figuring out if they apply right now, right here. And, if they apply, what precisely does that mean I should or should not do in this particular context?—for all rules, even ethical rules, tend to have their ambiguities.

If you believe what their friends say, the infamous figures in big corporate and government scandals are not bad people; they love their families and don't cheat at golf. But, somehow, the ethical alarms in their heads failed to go off or they found ways to quiet them. These once respected and admired people were ruined because their ethics didn't kick in to save them.

If the primary problem with ethics is in knowing when they apply, the secondary problem is that people don't always agree about them. You may think it's unethical to bribe suppliers to get preferred treatment, but some people would regard it as merely a cost of doing business. Some people may think it's unethical to charge personal expenses to a company expense account, but you might regard it as part of your compensation. The point is that you, as the manager, cannot rely on your own ethics or your employees' ethics to trigger alarm bells when you or they begin to do things that later will be cited as unethical. Every one of us has experienced too many ethical lapses of our own to fully trust our alarm systems, and we've read about too many lapses in newspapers and magazines to believe other people should trust theirs. Most of us intend to behave ethically, but it is a haunting certainty that every one of us will someday regret ethical lapses we haven't even committed yet.

Many organizations have decided that they cannot rely on the personal ethics of their managers and employees to ensure ethical behavior. Some have attempted to deal with this by requiring attendance at ethics training courses. If the goal of these programs is to teach ethics, they probably are too late; most of us learned our particular version of ethics when we were children. Moreover, most of us resent the implication that we are unethical, which is how ethics training is often interpreted. It's not surprising that these programs meet with resistance.

Of course, teaching people ethics doesn't necessarily teach them what they really need to know—when the ethics apply and how. In this sense, all the well-intended courses in the world aren't going to have much impact. Realizing this, many organizations have given up on ethics training, or have augmented it by creating documents, called *codes of ethics,* that provide guidelines about how employees are expected to behave in various kinds of situations. Because they are written to fit the organization as a whole, they usually focus on the big things—antitrust issues, environmental policies, government relations, international business, employee purchases and sales of the organization's stock, and corrupt practices like bribery, theft of intellectual and real property, and so on. Because of this focus, they often are insufficiently specific about the issues that are of particular importance to an individual unit. It therefore is a good idea to back up the organization's code of ethics with a unit-specific code that swaps the abstract talk about big things for concrete rules about little things: what is expected of employees in the ethically (and legally) dangerous situations that occur on the unit's level. In Chapter 5, we'll discuss how to write such a code for your unit.

What Employees Expect of You

Employees have fairly clear expectations about what the organization, and you, should contribute to their well-being as members of the organization and as members of your unit. Appropriate pay and benefits are among those expectations, but you probably have less control over them than you do over the other things they expect from their jobs, so we'll move on to the other things.

First, they have expectations about their jobs and what you should do to make sure those expectations are met. Second, they have expectations about you, personally, and the professional image you project—after all, you serve as the unit's representative to the larger organization and beyond, and they are concerned about how well you do it.

Expectations about Your Behavior

Employee expectations about their jobs can be grouped into six categories:

- They expect to have structure, stability, and a low level of uncertainty, so they expect you to be *organized.*
- They expect to have access to the information they need to do their jobs, so they expect you to *communicate.*
- They expect clear performance standards and for rewards to follow from conforming to those standards, so they expect you to provide *feedback.*
- They expect to be understood, to be allowed to express their thoughts and feelings, and to grow, so they expect you to be *supportive.*
- They expect to be valued, to feel a part of things, and to be an equal among their peers, so they expect you to be *fair.*
- They expect you and the other managers in the organization to exhibit *professionalism,* about which we'll say more in a moment.

As their manager, and as the agent of the organization with whom they have the most contact, your employees expect you to ensure that their job expectations are met. Moreover, they must see that you are trying and that you are succeeding, insofar as possible. If they think you aren't trying or that you might fail, they will feel threatened, become anxious, and strive to alleviate the threat or leave. If you try but fail, they will give you credit for trying but, ultimately, they'll be disappointed and strive to repair things or leave. Efforts to remove a threat and efforts to repair a failure are both likely to consist of trying to get you replaced.

Meeting employees' expectations while simultaneously striving to meet your boss's expectations as well as your own is a daunting task—not to be lightly undertaken and certainly not to be attempted without forethought. You really have to consider what your options are; your unit's operational environment within the organization places constraints on what you can and cannot do. Then you have to consider your own strengths and weaknesses; some of us aren't well suited to meeting others' expectations—we hardly can cope with our own—so perhaps we oughtn't get in the position of managing other people in the first place.

But, presuming you think you're up to the task, the first thing to realize is that you have to tailor your strategies to your individual employees; while they may all hold the same general expectations, the emphasis will be different for each of them. Thus, someone who places a priority on being a valued part of the group will require a slightly different approach than someone whose priority is the need for structure.

Nuances aside, however, your strategy should address each of the six categories of expectations listed above by being organized, communicating openly, providing feedback, being supportive, being fair, and exhibiting professionalism. The relative emphasis placed on each of these, and the precise ways in which you go about doing them, depend on your appraisal of your employees' priorities, both individually and as a group, as well as organizational constraints upon what you can do.

Research shows that when employees are asked to compare their expectations of their manager's behavior with the manager's actual behavior, the greater the rated disparity between the two, the greater their dissatisfaction with the manager and the more likely they are to consider leaving the organization. On the other hand, the same research shows that employees are not unreasonable; they will tolerate a bit of disparity—a narrow zone within which they feel comfortable enough to regard their manager's efforts as sufficient, if not perfect. However, once the disparity exceeds that comfort zone, satisfaction quickly plunges and the inclination to leave quickly rises. That is, expectations can endure a little violation, but not much, before they turn into disappointment.

Finally, notice that the six categories of expectations held by your employees are the same as your own expectations, and the behavior they expect of you is the same as you expect of your boss. You should heed the Manager's Golden Rule, "Do unto your employees as you would have your boss do unto you."

Professionalism

Let's expand on the sixth category of employee expectations, professionalism. Employees, and your boss, expect you to behave as a professional and to maintain a professional image—that is, look like a professional. And they don't want you to fake it; they want the real thing. On the other hand, although they don't want you to try to be someone you aren't, they don't want to be embarrassed by you. The following are a few pointers about how to meet their expectations without having to pretend.

Behavior

Your employees expect you to behave like the professional you are (or you wouldn't be their manager). This doesn't mean being officious or bustling around trying to look efficient, which usually ends up as a laughable parody of professionalism. What it means is that you exhibit your ability and confidence by:

- Being *competent* at your job and doing it in a timely manner;
- Being *consistent* in your expectations and in keeping your promises;
- Being as *open* as possible about the things that you do and explaining to those who are affected just what you are doing and why;
- Being *respectful* of employees who have experience and skill and listening to their advice;
- Being *courteous* without being overly formal;
- Being *modest* about your role in the unit's successes and giving appropriate credit to your employees;
- Being *aware* of your strengths and weaknesses, building on the former and finding ways to overcome the latter.

Don't panic, nobody expects you to be superhuman or a paragon of virtue. People merely expect you to try to be a decent person and to behave in a manner that befits, and enhances, your position as their manager.

Image

In addition to behaving professionally, your employees expect you to maintain a professional image.

Clothes. The rule for clothes is simple: Dress slightly more formally than your employees, but don't overdo it. That is, if the local dress standard is casual, dress casually with a couple of formal touches—wear a subdued tie or scarf, wear dress shoes instead of sneakers, and so on. If the standard is formal, pay just a little more for a little better quality, but don't flaunt it. Be fashionable, but not obviously so. Don't wear sexy clothes, not even on Casual Friday—this is work, not play. Tight is not right!

If you have difficulties selecting suitable clothes, hire a consultant to teach you, it's worth the expense.

Grooming. Be sparing with scent; your body adapts to the odor soon after applying it, so you often fail to realize how overpowering it can be. Cologne and aftershave should be a vague presence, not a dense cloud that might set off allergies or make eyes water. Hairstyle should be fashionable for your age, not too young and never outrageous. Tattoos should be modest and mostly covered up. For women, fingernails should be of reasonable length and not gaudily decorated. For men, facial hair should be modest and well trimmed; if you shave your head, do it regularly.

Attitude. Be upbeat, but not rah-rah. Slogans are intrinsically superficial, and spouting them makes you appear superficial too. Be friendly with your employees, but don't overstep the line. Never be condescending; treat your employees as you would want to be treated—you may be their manager, but they work for the organization, not for you personally. Strive to build a legacy for the manager who takes your place when you move up—a well-run unit with high morale.

Manners. Always try to be courteous. Abruptness causes more problems than it solves and makes you look like an ill-bred lout or an arrogant fool. On the other hand, don't be too stilted; drinking tea with an extended pinkie is as bad as slurping it. Never drink alcohol to excess around your employees—alcohol lowers inhibitions, and honesty isn't the best policy when you can't monitor what you're saying or doing. Being able to speak languages other than English is great, but it is rude to do so around people who do not share your ability; people become uncomfortable (and paranoid) in the presence of conversations they can't understand.

If you don't think your social skills are up to snuff, hire a consultant to teach you; again, it's worth the expense.

Speech. No matter how professionally you dress and behave, if you speak like a child, if you mumble or speak in an uninflected monotone, if you always seem to be apologizing or asking a question, or if your voice is harsh or raspy, all of your other efforts are in vain. Most of us have no idea how much our mode of speech influences the impression we make—and not just the first impression. To older persons, the repeated use of the word "like" makes the speaker sound like a child, perhaps resulting in an underestimation of his or her abilities. People who talk too loudly come off as overbearing and boorish; those who speak too softly come off as shy and apologetic. Mumbling makes you seem unassertive and shy. Speaking in a monotone, without appropriate inflection, puts listeners to sleep and sounds like a child reciting a poem for the grownups. Ending each declarative sentence with an upward inflection makes everything into a question, suggesting uncertainty and lack of decisiveness—and it's tedious to listen to. Talking nonstop is bullying, particularly if you're talking to an employee. If your voice sounds like fingernails on a blackboard, listeners will be so distracted by their cringing nerves that they won't hear what you're saying. If you have a strong regional accent or a problem with diction, listeners who are unaccustomed to it may have difficulty understanding you. And, while it's nice to have a large vocabulary, the needless use of big or obscure words doesn't impress anyone.

Nobody expects you to be a pargon of perfect speech—to sound like a TV newscaster or a Shakespearian actor, but it doesn't hurt to check yourself out and break bad habits. It won't do much good to ask your friends if you have faulty speech habits, because they're used to you, and they probably speak much the way you do anyway, so you'll sound fine to them. Instead, record your voice while reciting a poem, reading a passage from a book, and giving a short off-the-cuff talk on a topic of your choice. If things don't make much sense when you listen to the recording, or if you sound tentative, with questions where there weren't any, or if your voice sounds unpleasant, it is time to seek help. Speech coaches and speech therapists are easy to find, but you shouldn't trust just anyone. You might begin by calling the Speech and Hearing Department at the nearest college or university and asking for a recommendation—they often have clinics for speech training. Speaking well is an asset to your career, so whatever it costs to correct bad habits is a good investment in your future.

Summary

To ensure mastery of the material in this chapter, summarize it for yourself by filling in this topic outline.

I. What Expectations Do _____

_____

   A. Expectations and Scenarios _____

_____

   B. Threats _____

_____

   C. Beliefs and Values _____

_____

D. Violations _____

_____

II. "Hot Buttons" _____

_____

III. Expectations in the Workplace _____

_____

    A. Dealing with Violations _____

    _____

        1. Grievance _____

        _____

        2. Leaving _____

        _____

        3. Revision of Violated Expectations _____

        _____

    B. Dealing with Threats _____

    _____

        1. Prevention _____

        _____

        2. Leaving _____

        _____

        3. Revision of Threatened Expectations _____

        _____

    C. Implications _____

    _____

    D. Presumed Obligations _____

    _____

IV. Beliefs, Values, and Ethics _____

_____

    A. Unethical Behavior _____

    _____

V. What Employees Expect of You

_____

A. Expectations about Your Behavior _____

_____

B. Professionalism _____

_____

   1. Behavior _____

_____

   2. Image _____

_____

Exercises

1. Return to each of the three managers you previously interviewed with questions derived from the material in this chapter. Ask what he or she knows about hot buttons and how to deal with them. Also ask about expectations and what happens when they are violated. Include at least one question about ethics and how ethical issues are dealt with in his or her organization. Because different organizations have different standards for what is regarded as professional behavior and image, ask your interviewees to describe the standards in their organizations.

2. Write an essay outlining your views on managing employees, incorporating what you have learned from the text and what you learned in your interviews.

3. Add your essay to your notebook.

Sources and Further Reading

Beach, L.R. (Ed.) (1996). *Decision making in the workplace: A unified perspective.* Mahwah, NJ: Erlbaum.

Bissell, B.R. (1992). *Relationship between incongruity between supervisory strategy and satisfaction with the organization and/or supervision.* Unpublished Ph.D. dissertation, University of Arizona.

Dennet, D.C. (2006). *Breaking the spell: Religion as a natural phenomenon.* New York: Viking Penguin.

4

Anticipating Emotions

*Good managers commit to anticipating the emotions
that arise from threatened or violated expectations
and to dealing with them constructively.*

In the preceding chapter (Chapter 3), we discussed how threatened or violated expectations give rise to emotions and, in turn, how these emotions motivate preventive or ameliorative actions or attempts to escape. In this chapter, we are going to focus on those emotions and the actions they prompt, as well as constructive ways of dealing with them.

Working together involves close interaction between both the manager and his or her employees, and among employees themselves. Because the vagaries of human interaction frequently result in threatened or violated expectations, emotions are a normal part of the picture. However, normal though they may be, emotions can cause difficulties, so you must be aware of them, and how to deal with them, so they don't have a disproportional impact on decisions and actions.

Drama and Trauma

Like every other human, you are programmed through genetics and experience to react to your own and to others' emotions. As a result, it is easy to find yourself swamped by emotional demands. The key to handling these demands is to identify the emotions that have only transitory effects, which we will call drama, and those that will have lasting and deleterious effects, which we will call trauma.

Drama

Drama doesn't require you to do much of anything, because it is an expression of momentary emotions; however intense, things will settle down soon.

In fact, because drama usually involves someone letting off steam about threatened or violated expectations, it can be a good thing; the person can get it out of his or her system and move on. The trick is to be accepting of the dramatic emotional outburst without being manipulated by it. You don't necessarily have to do anything to stop it, and you don't necessarily have to solve the problem that brought it on—frequently there isn't anything you can do anyway, so save your energy. Most important, don't try to purchase serenity by offering something to make the person feel better. Peace offerings are condescending, and it's silly to treat someone like a child with a skinned knee whose parent offers an ice-cream cone if they'll just stop crying. It is far better to let the drama play itself out. Think of it as theater rather than as a problem to be solved. It will pass; your job is simply to see that it doesn't leave any lasting damage.

For example, when an employee storms into your office raving about having been treated badly by a customer, you know it is merely drama. Both you and the employee know you can't hunt down the customer and demand an apology and a promise to reform—and you wouldn't if you could. In fact, you can't do anything but listen and make sympathetic noises. The employee merely needs to blow off steam to someone who might be able to do something, although he or she doesn't really expect you to. Your only job here is to see that the employee's emotions don't result in ill treatment of the customer during their next encounter.

To regard certain behavior as simply drama is not to say it is trivial to the person involved. The person may feel very strongly, and the emotions may last for a long time. Drama merely means that you can't or shouldn't do anything in reaction to the emotions. Your only real responsibility, aside from listening, is to prevent bad side effects. Emotional drama washes over everybody in the vicinity, and well-meaning and sympathetic bystanders may take it upon themselves to remedy things. For example, well-meaning coworkers may feel moved to instruct the rude customer about how to behave or get revenge by rendering poor service or insulting the customer themselves. This sort of thing is damaging to the unit, and it is your job to prevent it.

Let's be clear: drama isn't limited to your employees. You too have emotional outbursts that don't necessarily require action; you just need to blow off steam. When this happens, make sure you unload your emotions and your steam somewhere else. On those days when you're fed up and out of sorts, and something gets under your skin, work off your pent-up anger, stress, or guilt (or all three) safely away from the workplace. Go to the gym, go running, go bowling, meditate, work on your stamp collection, but don't blow up at your employees, yell at your spouse and kids, kick the dog, drive recklessly, or pick a fight in a bar. Learning to handle the drama of your own emotions is an important part of maturing as well as being crucial to being a good manager.

Trauma

Trauma is different from drama because you can and should do something. When emotions run high enough to have a lasting negative impact on the person, his or her coworkers, or the unit, you have to intervene. In some cases the emotional person is you, and in some cases it is an employee, but either way, something must be done to prevent traumatic consequences for the unit's performance and for the people involved. In what follows, we will examine emotionality that has the potential for trauma, and how to deal with it.

Fear

Fear is a reaction to a real or imagined threat to one's expectations. It always surprises me how fearful the workplace is for some people. Often it is fear of failure and the humiliation of being reprimanded. Sometimes it is fear of success and the possibility of being given even harder tasks, eventually being given something too hard and then failing. Quite often it is fear of being unmasked—revealed to be less confident, less competent, and less intelligent than one thinks others expect one to be. Whatever its causes, fear tends to make employees (and managers) conservative. The result is that they are less innovative, because innovations don't always work and therefore are threatening. They are less responsible, because taking responsibility means taking heat if things go wrong, which is threatening. They are resistant to changes, because change is unfamiliar, and therefore threatening. In short, they become extremely resistant to anything involving risk, because risk, which means a threat of failure, evokes even more fear than they had in the first place. Much of what people refer to as "stress" actually is fear.

I have known people who were in a constant, unrelenting state of fear stemming from their jobs. I had a secretary who was convinced she couldn't live up to her own expectations about her job performance, in spite of my constant reassurances that she was doing very well. As a result, anything short of lavish praise was interpreted as a criticism and a sign that she had fallen short. It was very tedious, but eventually she became more confident and ended up working in the job, for a succession of managers, for twenty years.

Fear isn't just for employees. I knew the business manager of a large institution who had the reputation for being a very difficult boss. He was unrelenting in his criticism of his staff, making them work long hours and insisting on work being done over until it met his high expectations. What his fearful staff didn't know was that his harshness was driven by his own fear that he couldn't meet his high expectations about his job performance, and he refused to let any laxness on their part further imperil what he regarded as his already tenuous hold on things. The result was a strange mixture of aggressiveness with his employees and timidity with his own boss. His employees despised him as a tyrant, his boss despised him as a wimp, and he despised himself as a fraud. It was a miserable situation all around.

Sometimes, of course, fear is exactly the right reaction under the circumstances. The employees of our business manager were right to quake in fear of him, even as they despised him. He was notorious for verbally abusing and firing people who didn't meet his exacting standards. However, passive quaking is not the usual reaction to fear; more commonly it arouses a feeling of being treated unjustly, which leads to anger, which can lead to resistance, revenge, and sabotage. If this was the reaction of the employees of the manager about whom we've been talking, his fear about failing to meet his own expectations would be justified; angry employees' resistance, revenge, and sabotage would make it nearly impossible for him to do his job well.

Anger

Anger occurs when there is a discrepancy between how an employee expects to be treated and how you or others actually are treating him or her. Thus, for example, if the employee agrees that his or her performance is poor and that he or she might do better in a different job, your decision to transfer him or her will not evoke anger. If, however, he or she thinks the poor performance is not attributable to anything he or she did or didn't do, he or she will see being transferred as unjust and will become angry.

In nature, anger usually precedes threats of violence, which aim to counteract threats to oneself, or actual violence, which aims to force changes in bad events that already have happened or to get revenge for them. In the workplace, however, violence is discouraged, and is usually replaced by disciplinary actions or dismissals. As a result, anger in the workplace seldom implies physical violence; it implies organizationally sanctioned punishment.

Anger in the workplace serves another, more subtle purpose—conveying information. When anger is unexpressed, so it is known only to the angry person, it informs that person about how much he or she cares about the threatened or violated expectation, usually because it derives from important beliefs and values. When anger is expressed, it informs both the angry person and everybody else about how much he or she cares about the threatened or violated expectation. How much he or she cares is revealed by the intensity of the anger.

Unexpressed anger may dissipate over time if expectations change, making the discrepancy decrease. If it doesn't dissipate, the resentment that builds up may find outlet in inappropriate ways—taking it out on innocent bystanders (Freud called this displacement) or internalizing it to the disadvantage of one's health (he called this repression). Much of what people call stress in the workplace is this bottled-up anger; you're all fired up to be violent, and you can't, so you stoically endure the tension that it produces. You feel awful, but you keep going because there doesn't seem to be anything else to do. This is what keeps psychotherapists in business.

Expressed anger is a form of bullying, because it always carries the threat that actual violence is possible if things don't go the way the angry person wants them to. Even when violence is unlikely, most people react to others' anger as though it was in fact a threat, and they react to that threat by:

- Counter-anger, which means blunting the angry person's threat with their own threat;
- Leaving the scene;
- Appeasement, which means doing what the angry person wants them to do.

Because we know that people react in this way, most of us use expressed anger as a way of bullying them into doing what we want, even when we have no intention of causing them physical harm. That is, we play on their almost instinctive reaction to anger in the hope of inducing them to appease us by changing their behavior. Of course, anger usually evokes counter-anger in an attempt to curb its implied threat. But if we refuse to be intimidated by that counter-anger, the threatened person is left with only two options, leaving the scene or appeasement. If leaving is impossible or the price of doing so is greater than the price of appeasing, appeasement is the only option left, which is what the strategic anger was aimed at achieving in the first place.

You

It may seem extreme to equate expressed anger and bullying, but it's true. Bullying is defined as using violence and threats of violence to make people do what you want them to do. Managers who are quick to anger exert control over their employees by threatening to unleash their rage—which implies violence or at least punishment. By staying on the brink, they use anger as a weapon to bully the people around them into either quitting or appeasing their demands.

Explosive and Strategic Anger

Expressed anger can be divided into two categories, explosive and strategic. Explosive anger—temper tantrums, flying off the handle, losing it—results from a loss of control. It usually is destructive because:

- You end up doing and saying things that you later regret—strident accusations and extravagant threats;
- It vividly demonstrates to your employees (and everyone else) that you are immature, controlled by your emotions rather than reason. You clearly are not the kind of strong, in-charge person they need you to be;
- It leaves nothing in reserve. Explosive anger demands immediate results, and if they don't happen, you don't have much left short of punishment. Punishment following explosive anger will be seen as vengeance rather than justice; it may hurt the punished people, but it won't really change them and it will undermine your legitimacy in the eyes of their coworkers.

Strategic anger differs from explosive anger in that it is always under control. It too is bullying, but it is intentional and precise bullying. It is the result of a conscious decision to let others know that you are displeased by the violation of your expectations. It signals that you care, that you are intent on changing things, and that they can cooperate or they can take the consequences—which are implied if not wholly spelled out. Strategic anger forcefully focuses attention on the problem, makes it clear that you intend for changes to occur that solve the problem, and implies that failure to change will have repercussions. It is strategic bullying, but bullying nonetheless.

An example of strategic anger: The head of one of the sections of a unit I supervised insisted on submitting budget requests that were so unrealistic that I had to send them back to be pared down. This happened repeatedly; she'd submit and I'd send it back, over and over. All the while, work on my unit's annual budget request came to a stop while we waited to integrate her request. I tried to explain that we had a deadline, but she seemed not to hear. It was as though she was trying to wear me down so I'd accept her inflated budget—which simply wasn't going to happen. In fact, our impasse was just the latest in a series of concerns I'd had with her performance as section head; she really was not very good, but her employees didn't realize it yet. I could have removed her from her job, but I had nobody to replace her and, although she wasn't good, she wasn't dreadful. I figured it was better to wait until her employees became disenchanted before removing her (which soon happened, leading her to resign).

After the budget conflict had been going on for nearly a month, I decided that I had to do something drastic to get through to her. At our next meeting I intentionally allowed my anger show. It wasn't difficult, because I really was angry. After we had had our usual fruitless discussion, I stood, looked straight at her, and let my voice become hard as I told her that this had to stop, that I was at the end of my patience, that it was her job to recognize the unit's needs as well as her section's, and that failure to respond to my requests would force me to write a budget request for her, one that would not please her. (Note that I didn't threaten to replace her because at the moment I hadn't anybody and she knew it.)

Her immediate reaction was counter-anger accompanied by an attempt to escape by changing the topic. She began with a series of defensive "Yes, but . . ." statements followed by a list of all the perceived injustices done to her and her section over the previous few years. I let her spout off for a while, then I interrupted and, in the same hard voice as before, told her that her complaints were irrelevant to the problem at hand (which was true) and that we could discuss them at a later date, but I wasn't there to negotiate. Quite the contrary, my only concern was a reasonable budget request and I wanted it on my desk by noon of the following day or I would whip something together myself. An acceptable request was submitted early the next morning.

My relationship with the section head was never very good after I bullied her with my strategic anger, but it was good enough. More important, it established an understanding between us; I was in charge, and when I made a request it was to be taken seriously. I would entertain discussion and disagreement, but ultimately, I made the decisions because I had to look out for the welfare of the entire unit, of which her section was only a part.

Strategic anger should be reserved for special occasions. It declares that negotiation is over and you've moved on to threats. Moreover, it implies that if threats don't work, you are prepared to do what you threatened to do. If, in fact, you are not ready to carry through, your use of strategic anger is simply a bluff. If the bluff doesn't work, you will have to reopen negotiations, and this time around you will be negotiating from a considerably weaker position.

Them

Employees also become angry when their expectations aren't met. As we saw in Chapter 3, employees come to expect to be treated in particular ways as part of an obligation the organization has to them; a sort of implicit contract between them and the organization. When they think that contract has been violated, they become angry. Sometimes they keep their anger to themselves, but it eventually has repercussions. Sometimes they express their anger, either explosively or strategically, in an effort to induce you to acknowledge the contract violation and to do something about it.

Often employees' anger is justified; they actually have been poorly treated. In this case, your job is to make amends in some way. On the other hand, anger as a reaction to your attempts to solve performance problems cannot be appeased; you have to solve the problem. The tactic here is to try to change the employees' expectations or change their interpretation of what you've done, in an effort to reduce or eliminate the anger—often this can be accomplished through explanations and apologies.

Unfortunately, real or perceived injustices go beyond the person who supposedly has been mistreated. Coworkers, friends, family, and the general public can be roused to anger by perceived violations of what they believe employees have a right to expect from you and the organization. Again, it is your job to make amends when it is appropriate to do so. If it isn't, you must try to change their expectations or change their interpretation of what was done. Again, the key lies in explanations and/or apologies.

Explanations and Apologies

I know of no society in which it is sufficient to merely announce the way in which a real or perceived injustice is to be repaired without appending an explanation and, in some cases, a statement of regret. Rules of social interaction demand more, and most of us feel decidedly uncomfortable when we violate those rules. Moreover, everybody involved—the person, coworkers, and bystanders—expects more, and they don't feel that things are complete unless more is provided. This feeling of incompleteness leads to harsh reactions; a feeling of the person having been demeaned, humiliated, given short shrift, treated shabbily, all of which engender negative attitudes and behavior.

When restitution cannot be made (and even when it can), there are two ways to avoid or reduce people's feelings of being treated badly: explanations and apologies. Both of them are largely symbolic, but they mean a lot to the people who receive them and they often have redemptive value for the people who give them. As a result, they play an important role in bringing closure.

Explanations

Scientists have examined the nature of explanations given by those whose actions adversely affect another person. In the present case, we will limit ourselves to the case in which a manager's actions caused or will cause real harm to an employee.

There are four kinds of explanations you can give for action that adversely affects an employee:

- Clichés such as "Stuff happens!" or "That's life," rather than any details about what necessitates the action.
- Citation of specific rules the person has violated that necessitates the action.
- A "big picture" description of the larger forces that necessitate the action.
- Narratives involving the people, events, and repercussions that logically led to the action.

Clichés convey virtually no information and do not properly serve as an explanation—their main purpose is to prevent any further discussion. When you resort to clichés, you are telling the person that you do not feel obliged to account for your actions and that you do not care how he or she feels about it. Managers sometimes resort to clichés because they feel guilty about having taken action but are unwilling to reveal those feelings; clichés halt the discussion in its tracks and allow the manager to escape. (In some cases, the manager may be too inarticulate to give a real explanation and resorts to clichés simply because he or she feels that something—anything—has to be said.) Unfortunately, clichés, which may serve well in casual conversation, almost always fail as explanations for actions whose consequences are too severe to be blown off with flip remarks. The employee who hears a cliché instead of a real explanation will feel far more wronged than if the manager had said nothing at all.

Citation of specific rules (the organization's or your expectations) that the employee has violated may be an adequate justification for an action, but it is regarded by most people as coldly legalistic and somewhat brutal if that is the only explanation. Most of us believe that justice must be tempered with a little humanity. Rules can be mechanical and inflexible, people can be flawed and fallible. Unless rule violation leads to significantly serious consequences, or unless it represents the latest in a series of violations, most of us do not regard drastic retribution as reasonable or fair. We need more than just rule breaking as a reason to cause the culprit extreme distress and hardship.

Exactly what constitutes a "big picture" description of the forces leading to your action depends on the circumstances. If you are disciplining a person for improper behavior, the big picture might involve a discussion of how social functioning depends on each person making a contribution, working with others, etc., etc. The goal would be to show how the person's behavior violated his or her coworkers' rightful expectations and thus constitutes a failure to be a contributing and valued member of the unit. This kind of explanation has more of a "human face" than clichés or rule citation, but it still is a little cold. Most people find it acceptable as an explanation, but not wholly satisfying.

A narrative explanation depicts the people who were involved in the events that created the problem for which action is being taken, when and where those events occurred, how they affected other people, and why they necessitate the action. This explanation puts an even greater "human face" on things because it focuses on specific people and specific events, explores the events' impacts on those people, and puts responsibility for the harm that was done upon the employee. It creates a justifiable reason for your action in terms of damage to other people, to the unit, and to the organization. This kind of explanation makes the most sense to most people, and it can be the most satisfying. However, narratives are merely stories, and as such they leave out some things and stress others and offer opportunities for factual error. Indeed, most narratives could be told in a number of different ways and still claim to be as accurate as the one you tell. This fact makes it reasonably easy to challenge the way you tell the story or the accuracy of its details. Even though the challenge may not actually refute the story, it can cast doubt on it and, by extension, on the legitimacy of the action you are taking. If the person (and his or her advocates) believes your version, the narrative probably will be regarded as a satisfactory explanation and may do much to reduce feelings of being mistreated. If they don't believe it, the feelings of injustice and indignation are intensified. Narrations as explanations, while they can be quite satisfying, must be used carefully or they can make things worse than they might have been with one of the other kinds of explanations.

Apologies

Effective apologies are based on empathy and sympathy.

Empathy is the ability to put yourself in the other person's place, to imagine how you would feel if what is happening to him or her were happening to you. People who are unable to empathize tend to treat other people badly because it doesn't occur to them that they are being hurtful or mean.

Empathy is a two-edged sword for managers. Without it, you'd probably act like a tyrant, never giving a second thought to how your actions affect your employees. On the other hand, if you anticipate every negative feeling your employees might experience, you are apt not to act when you should.

The fact is you cannot manage employees without making some of them unhappy some of the time. You may go out of your way to be fair, to help them in every possible way, to go the extra mile for them, but there always will be cases in which your best efforts fail. There always will be employees who cannot or will not do what is expected of them. When this happens, you must take action, and that action often causes the person to be unhappy. The fact that you can anticipate this unhappiness, and the fact that you would very much dislike feeling it yourself, is not a reason for inaction. The problem will not go away just because you don't want to make anyone feel unhappy, uncomfortable, or unloved.

Sympathy is empathy with the other person's distress combined with a desire to alleviate it, even if you can't. If an employee's son is killed in an accident, you can imagine how awful he must feel, you can yearn to help the employee feel less miserable, but there really is nothing you can do. In these circumstances, most of us make do with an expression of sympathy (usually, "I'm so sorry for your loss . . .") and a sincere, but usually futile, expression of our desire to alleviate the hurt if we could (". . . and if there is anything I can do, please call on me").

Managers need both empathy and sympathy—the first helps us understand what others experience, and the second motivates us to help when we can, or at least to express caring, which is a valued social gesture. But, just as empathy can cause trouble if it leads to inaction, sympathy can cause trouble if it leads to inappropriate action. It makes no sense to discipline an employee if you turn right around and undo it because you sympathize with how awful the discipline makes him or her feel. Even expressing sympathy beyond the usual social niceties ("I'm sorry I have to do this, but . . .") can undo the lesson the disciplining is designed to teach. Even if you feel absolutely wretched and your heart cries out to ease the person's pain, you must not do it or you will negate the very thing you are trying to accomplish.

Of course, I'm not telling you to be hardhearted or cruel. But discipline accompanied by expressions of sympathy sends conflicting messages. Moreover, if you discipline someone, how likely is it that they will believe your expression of sympathy? You'll simply look hypocritical or weak. If you are so affected by the consequences of your disciplinary actions, perhaps you have been overly harsh in your choice of actions, and you should think things through again; but, don't turn back simply out of sympathy. On the other hand, if after taking action you find there is sufficient reason (and your guilt feelings are not a sufficient reason) to believe that you have acted in error or too harshly, you must consider whether to apologize and whether to make restitution.

An apology is an acknowledgment that you have acted unjustly and that you feel bad about it. The goal is to restore the dignity and self-respect of the offended person as well as to restore your relationship to something approximating what it was prior to your unjust action. When your action resulted in the unjust departure of an employee, the apology may not be offered to the offended person at all—he or she is gone—but it may be offered to the remainder of the group in an effort to restore trust and reassure them that you want to behave fairly, even if you sometimes make mistakes.

The first thing to remember about apologizing is that you shouldn't do it unless you mean it. Sincerity is a necessity. Anything less makes the apology an insult and only makes a bad situation worse. Oh sure, people say, "I'm sorry" for all sorts of things for which they aren't in the least sorry—"I'm sorry, but would you pass the butter?" Used this way, what might appear to be an apology actually is merely a social convention—a way of acknowledging that you expect someone to go a little out of their way for you. In fact, the word "sorry" probably isn't very valuable; it's used so easily and so frequently that it hasn't much meaning.

In addition to sincerity, a real apology should include an explanation of the circumstances that led you to make the decision to act as you did and why you now regard that decision as flawed. Then you must acknowledge the distress the action caused the person and your feelings (guilt, remorse, shame) about having been the instigator of their distress. Finally, you must offer some sort of restitution, real or symbolic.

Sometimes restitution is straightforward. If the unjust action resulted in financial distress, then pairing the apology with compensation may be acceptable. If the action deprived the person of opportunities, then pairing the apology with efforts to reinstate the opportunities or create new ones may be acceptable. However, if real restitution is impossible because the damage was intangible, the apology can serve as a symbolic restitution. For example, if the action besmirched the person's reputation or diminished his or her standing with coworkers, then the apology may be all you can do, but it must be public so others can see that person was wronged. Public apologies are hard for most of us because they make us look inept and foolish. But, if you do something unjust to someone, something that humiliates them, you may indeed have been inept and foolish and you might as well admit it—everybody probably knows it anyway. They will be more willing to forgive you and let things get back to normal if you do the honorable thing and sincerely apologize.

Of course, unjust decisions often are the result of mistakes and misinformation, and it is appropriate to include these as mitigating factors in your apology, but you must do so carefully. If you cite other people or untoward events as causes of your flawed decision, you had better be convincing or it will look like you are trying to weasel out of taking blame. Nothing destroys an apology more thoroughly than weaseling—and it leaves you in worse repute with everyone than you were before. Even if outside factors actually are to blame, it sometimes is better not to even mention them, rather than risk appearing to be weaseling. Apologize, take the blame, and endure the repercussions. Allow everyone to forgive you—they'll feel magnanimous and you can all get back to work.

Hatred and Violence

When anger grows into hatred, the implied threat contained in anger may escalate into real actions, even in the workplace, where they are forbidden. There is a gradation of hateful acts. Some are merely mean, petty things, the goal of which is to distress the hated person or threaten his or her security. These are disquieting and disruptive, but they are not as serious as acts that inflict actual pain and physical damage. When the unit's performance is threatened, even petty acts must be addressed, but violent acts can never go unchallenged.

Just witnessing hate and hateful behavior is almost as distressing as being its target. Hate is coercive to everyone around it because, even in petty cases, it causes an undercurrent of uneasiness. This gets worse as the hate escalates, resulting in jarring eruptions, continuous friction and squabbling, and, then, outright violence. You can't be responsible for everyone liking each other and being nice, but anything beyond a mild undercurrent demands your attention, and even a mild undercurrent bears watching.

When hateful behavior comes to your attention, your first response must be to keep it from escalating into violence. Workplace violence is of three kinds:

- Violence directed by an outsider against an employee—for example, a distressed husband who assaults his wife, who is your employee.
- Violence directed by an employee against another employee—often someone who has worked closely with the victim and who feels wronged by the victim.
- Violence directed against a group of people—newspapers call it "going postal"—usually a disgruntled employee seeking revenge for real or perceived injustices at the hands of coworkers or the organization.

In the case of the outsider, the enmity frequently was there to see, if only in hindsight; the victim's marital problems were ongoing, and she may have discussed them with coworkers. In the case of employee-on-employee violence, it probably was there to see if anybody looked; the employee had it in for the guy he or she worked with, and the violence was just the next step in an ascending series of clashes. In the case of violence against a group, the hatred often is hidden. Unless you knew the employee very well, you might not have known how angry and full of hate he or she had become until the blowup happened. Hidden hatred, suddenly revealed, is somehow more frightening than obvious hatred, if only because it seems that the victim(s) couldn't have prevented it.

An astonishing number of assaults occur in the workplace each year, and homicide has become a major cause of work-related death. You probably can't keep a distraught husband or boyfriend from killing one of your employees, but you can see that your unit is as well protected as possible by the organization's security safeguards and ensuring that no weapons are brought into the workplace. On the other hand, you can detect potential violence by employees against employees by following a few guidelines.

Employee-on-employee violence usually is the end point in a series of altercations, starting small and growing, sometimes quite quickly. Hatred often starts with little things—the original annoyance, slight, insult, or injustice may be forgotten, but the anger stays, and grows into hatred. Usually, coworkers are aware of this hatred; they've seen the earlier clashes, and they recognize the growing intensity. The problem is that they may not regard it as their business to let anyone know what is going on, perhaps out of fear of becoming involved, but often out of a feeling that telling is tattling, and tattling as wrong. The only way for the organization to deal with this is through a clearly stated policy forbidding violence (in even its mildest forms) and a strong message that failure to inform is the same as being complicit, and the consequences should be clearly spelled out. You don't want to make people so paranoid that they report every squabble and disagreement, but you want them to understand that the organization is responsible for employee safety and that it cannot meet that responsibility without employee cooperation.

Upon being informed about a violent happening, you must call upon the problem-solving and decision-making skills you will acquire in the next two chapters (Chapters 5 and 6). Talk with everybody, decide if you have a problem, and, if so, is it serious. If the answer is "yes" in both instances, review the actions open to you to solve the problem, select one, and implement it. Throughout the process, your manager, Human Resources, and the lawyers must be kept informed. If the violence is extreme, beyond a loud argument, you should ask that they take over—they should be better versed in the legal issues and in how to deal with law enforcement.

Experts disagree on whether it is possible to spot potentially violent employees ahead of time. Those who think it is possible have proposed various behavior profiles, personality inventories, and the like, but it isn't clear if any of them are valid predictors. The proposals that strike me as most reasonable and most useful are simply lists of things to look out for as precursors to violence. Examples of common indicators are:

- Past history of violence
- History of drug or substance abuse
- Crisis in personal life
- Erratic behavior
- Mood swings
- Excessive stress and anxiety
- Unreliability and attendance problems
- Standoffishness
- Chip on shoulder
- Aggressiveness, yelling, slamming doors
- Negative attitudes, disgruntlement, antisocial behavior
- Paranoia
- Inappropriate displays of anger
- Explicit threats and abusive language, usually directed at coworkers

In short, just about anything that indicates a very unhappy, distressed person who seems incapable of coping with his or her problems can be of concern. The problem is, lots of people exhibit some or all of this list of warning signs and only an infinitesimally small number of them will ever become violent.

About all you can do is watch for extreme and suspicious behavior. If you have any influence on the person, you can try to get him or her into counseling, but you have to be careful—someone's mental health is their own business, not yours. There is no law against being weird, stressed, ill-tempered, or unsocial. Unless you can demonstrate clearly that these characteristics interfere in some way with job performance, it technically isn't any of your business. But it never hurts to keep your eye on things, just in case—and to keep your boss and Human Resources informed.

Stress

It has been observed by someone famous, I don't recall who, that anything worth doing involves stress. This is because worthwhile endeavors usually are somewhat risky. Risk is threatening because, by definition, we can't control the outcomes. The anxiety that results from a lack of control is known as "stress."

It may seem too simple to suggest that stress results from lack of control, but if you think about it, you'll see that it pretty much covers things. When you're overscheduled and rushing, you don't feel wholly in control and you feel stressed. When you have a task you don't know how to do, you don't feel in control and you feel stressed. When you are caught in the middle, between your manager's expectations and your employees' expectations, you don't have control and you feel stressed. In fact, I can't think of any stressful situation in which the contributing factor isn't a lack of control, or at least the perception of a lack of control.

Stress isn't necessarily bad. The greater the discrepancy between your expectations (in the sense of what you think should happen) and reality, the higher your level of stress. The more stress you feel, the more you are motivated to do something about it. For small discrepancies, stress may be too low to motivate you to do anything, which is okay. At medium levels it motivates you to calmly work on correcting the situation, which is good. Unfortunately, at high levels it is dysfunctional because it interferes with your ability to think and act in a deliberate manner, which is bad. So, even though you want to correct things, high stress makes you unable to focus well enough to do so. Prolonged high stress has deleterious effects on mental and physical health, and it induces irritability and short temperedness, both of which increase interpersonal conflict, which increases the stress even more.

Some people seem to seek fairly high levels of stress; they profess to hate the stress itself, but they clearly like what it tells them about themselves. I call these folks "stress junkies" because they use stress as a way of measuring how well they are doing their jobs—if they're stressed, they must be doing well.

A true stress junkie takes pride in being stressed. I once attended a luncheon organized by a group of public relations specialists. Before things began, each person introduced themself. Every one of them emphasized how overworked, busy, and stressed they were. But, in the telling, each of them saw the struggle as heroic and wore their stress like a badge of honor. It was like being in a hospital ward with all the patients competing to be the sickest.

Stress junkies often rationalize their addiction as a way of "keeping their edge." They are convinced that if they relax, their skills will atrophy, their ability to compete will disappear, and their careers will disintegrate. Of course, this little theory never gets tested because they stay stressed to "stay in the game." You simply can't reason with them. Any expression of concern about their perpetual stress is taken as a compliment, an affirmation of their dedication and motivation. It is hopeless; you can only stand by and wait for them to burn out.

You

If you are a normal person who doesn't want to live with unnecessary stress, you have to keep things in perspective. Not every discrepancy between your expectations and reality is a crisis. Sometimes it is not very important. Sometimes it is simply interesting, funny, or weird. And sometimes it makes you think in new and creative directions. Echoing our discussion at the beginning of this chapter, I recommend that you learn to sort events into either of two categories. One category is for drama—problems that are important enough for you to know about but that you can't solve or are not so important that you must rush to solve them. The other category is for trauma—problems that are truly serious and that you'd better solve, fast.

The trick is to keep a balance—otherwise you'll put everything in the trauma category and you'll bury yourself in stress. You have some control over the categorization; most events aren't clearly one or the other. Fear of failing to spot an important problem argues for calling most things trauma. Fear of stressing out argues for calling most of them drama. You have to figure out your priorities: risk versus sanity.

Of course, there are additional ways of coping with stress. Exercise helps some people, as do hobbies and all the rest of the things you'll find listed in the endless parade of articles on stress management in magazines and newspapers. Probably the most important thing, aside from maintaining your perspective, is to maintain friendships outside the workplace. Don't talk about your job with these folks; get your mind on other things for a while. I think that maintaining friendships, as well as strong family ties, is the best safeguard against becoming a stress junkie because the work required to maintain good friendships and family ties doesn't leave enough left over for being a junkie too.

Them

Your employees' stress has three sources: inability to control their jobs, inability to control their relationships with their coworkers, and inability to control their manager—that is, you.

Reduction of disruptive job-induced stress begins by making sure the flow of work is either below the employee's threshold for stress or is in some way within his or her control, so the employee can match the demand to his or her ability to do the work. Remember, people have limits—limits to how smart they are, limits to how fast they can work, limits to how well they handle being pushed to perform. You, as manager, must learn to appraise each employee's limits, working to expand those limits when they cause performance problems, but respecting them as a characteristic of the employee as a person. Of course, if the limits fall far short of what is required, and if those limits do not expand with time and help, you must decide what to do.

Pushing employees' limits will induce stress, but the trick is to figure out how much stress will motivate them and how much will debilitate them. By assessing their limits and gently pushing for the expansion of those limits while providing both the tools and training to help this happen, you can improve their performance without burdening them with too much stress.

We talked about anger and violence earlier in this chapter, but short of these strong reactions are the more commonplace squabbles that arise when people work together. Reduction of disruptive relationship-induced stress begins by allowing subordinates freedom to work things out, to exercise control over their relationships and their squabbles—don't intervene too soon. It is part of the human condition to be irritated by those around us. This irritation sometimes erupts into squabbles that can interfere with the smooth operation of the unit. Your job is to do little or nothing until the squabble looks like it is going to harm the unit or until it has dragged on without progress on the part of the participants to resolve it. At this point, you need to step in and act as a mediator, if that is possible, or move the squabbling parties to new locations or new jobs in order to reduce the friction.

Be warned, however: workplace squabbles often resemble a family squabble. The moment you intervene, the combatants may unite against you, resenting your intrusion. The more personal the squabble, the greater the chances the two parties will find your intervention offensive—they won't think it is any of your business. If it is hurting the unit, however, you have to make them understand that the squabble isn't as personal as they think. They often fail to recognize the effects they're having on everyone else.

Reduction of manager-induced stress begins by identifying what you are doing that takes control away from your employees. Of course, it is your job to exercise control; you can't relinquish it all to them. But, if you are pushing people too hard (and, by the way, stress junkies are notorious for trying to push other people as hard as they push themselves), you must think through why you are doing it. Is it really necessary, or do you just think pushing is part of your job? In fact, is it actually impairing the unit's performance rather than improving it? Is it because this one employee is creating a bottleneck or in some other way failing to keep up with the rest of the unit? In short, is pushing helping, or should you try something else?

As we've said before, you are a major factor in your employees' work-lives, and what you do has a huge impact on them. If you behave badly, they become stressed. Because stress demands action, when they can't do anything to correct your bad behavior, their frustration builds. They either bottle up this frustration or direct it at inappropriate targets. Tempers flare and squabbles increase in number and severity. Before long those who can do so leave for other jobs. Those who remain become even more stressed by the changes their colleagues' departures bring about. More stress means more trouble, making the unit's performance hard to maintain.

Probably the most stress-inducing thing you can do is to supervise poorly. Employees have a pretty good idea about how you should do your job; they expect you to know what you are doing, to be firm, and to be fair. They'll cut you some slack in the short run, but if you continually violate their expectations, they are going to be stressed and they are going to do what they can to reduce that stress—often things you would prefer they didn't. Therefore, it behooves you to understand their expectations. If their expectations are appropriate, meet them. If they aren't appropriate, change them. Doing your job well is the best thing you can do for your employees and the best thing for keeping their stress within tolerable limits.

Of course, some of your employees may be stress junkies; it isn't limited to managers. My experience with these folks is that they welcome any stress you can give them and if you don't give them enough, they'll generate it for themselves. You'd think this would make them good workers, but it usually doesn't. They tend to be out of sync with the rest of the unit, working like beavers to turn out stuff nobody else is ready to use. They'll even elaborate their jobs to turn out stuff nobody wants, just to keep their stress level up. Or they'll take over parts of other people's jobs, which may be welcomed by the slothful but isn't by anyone else. Frankly, I would rather have an employee I have to push a little than to have a stress junkie; they're just too high maintenance. If you resist feeding their addiction and can prevent them from feeding it themselves at the expense of the unit, they soon will start searching for a more stressful job.

Grief

Of all the things one can't control, the death of someone near to you is perhaps the most stressful. The natural reaction to death is grief, which is a sequence of emotions rather than just a single emotion. The sequence is called the grief syndrome: denial, anger, bargaining, depression, and finally, acceptance. Not everyone experiences all of these emotions or in this order, but the emotions are nonetheless overwhelming and generally uncontrollable. Moreover, most authorities believe that it is best if grieving persons are allowed to go through their particular version of the grief syndrome in their own way in order to work through their loss.

You

If you're the grieving person, be kind to yourself and accept offers of help—your performance is bound to deteriorate and, while you may want to work to keep some semblance of normality in your life as you work through your loss, don't expect too much of yourself. Your employees will make allowances, as will your boss. If you don't pull out of it in a reasonable time, seek grief counseling.

Them

Because it is so overwhelming, grief nearly always has a negative impact on job performance. The impact of the death of an employee's close friend or family member is pretty much limited to that employee's performance, although there are ripple effects throughout the unit. The death of someone in the unit, on the other hand, impacts the performance of everyone in the unit; more so if the death results from violence and even more so if the violence occurs on the job.

In all cases, you must be prepared to accommodate grieving, both out of compassion and because you haven't got a choice—grieving will occur no matter what. First, you should convey your sincere condolences and assure the grieving employee(s) of your support. Then you should give them time to attend the funeral or memorial service. And you should lower your performance expectations until recovery is fairly complete. If an individual's grief does not appear to be lessening over time, you might suggest grief counseling, but do so tactfully; grieving is very personal and if the person is performing his or her job adequately, it isn't really any of your business—not officially anyway. If it was a coworker who died, you may want to arrange for grief counseling for your employees who want it, especially if the death was violent and/or it occurred at work. In any case, you must expect your unit's performance to be impaired for a while, and your efforts to get things back on track must be subtle and patient.

Finally, note that grief occurs with any big loss, not just death. People going through divorces sometimes exhibit grief, with the same impact on job performance. Someone who loses their job, whose house burns down or is destroyed in a storm, who is diagnosed with a serious illness, and the like, may experience grief and need time to recover.

Lust and Love

Let's end our discussion of emotions by examining a couple that aren't usually thought of as belonging in the workplace but always turn up there anyway. It is human nature to lust and, sometimes, to fall in love. Because coworkers spend so much time in each other's company, it is natural for romantic ties to form. If these relationships don't violate the organization's rules or cause productivity problems, they aren't really any of your business.

Many organizations have rules against romantic ties, but they are almost impossible to enforce. No one really knows what causes two people to be attracted to each other, least of all the two people. So, rules prohibiting it aren't likely to have much effect. On the other hand, the reasons for the rules are often sound, and the problems they are designed to prevent can be solved, after the fact, by a little clear thinking and some goodwill on everyone's part.

You

The primary reason for the rules is to prevent nepotism, which is giving favored treatment to someone who is in some way related to you. Most managers solve this problem by moving one or the other member of an involved couple to a job that ensures that favoritism can't occur.

Nepotism is most commonly the issue when the manager becomes involved with an employee. Manager-employee romance is not a good idea, but having said that, when it happens, the manager must take the initiative in making sure that there isn't the slightest hint of favoritism. Unfortunately, this usually means that the employee has to move to some other unit or, at the very least, be supervised (and have his or her performance evaluations done by) someone else.

No matter how hard you try to be fair, nobody will ever believe that your romantic partner is treated precisely like everybody else. If nothing else, it is assumed that you talk to each other after work and that you sometimes talk about work, so he or she has information that is unavailable to the other employees. This leads to jealousy, and it gets worse if there are suspicions of special treatment too—and there are bound to be suspicions of special treatment.

It isn't just that jealousy and suspicion degrade the work atmosphere, it also is hard on the person with whom you are involved. However innocent that may be, he or she may become socially isolated, become the butt of jokes and innuendo, and become the subject of rumors and malicious gossip. It simply isn't true that everybody loves a lover—they sometimes fear and envy them, and fear and envy can lead to pretty shabby treatment.

Shabby treatment is bound to be painful and stress inducing and may well affect the person's performance. Now you face the problem of dealing with that poor performance, and you can't show even the faintest sign of favoritism. This means you probably have to be a bit harsher than you normally would be just to avoid looking lenient, which isn't going to help your relationship. You can't ask the coworkers to stop picking on your loved one because it will look like you're making a special case and blaming them for what they see as a problem that you caused. You really are between a rock and a hard place.

And it can get worse. What happens if you break up? Now you're really in a bind; you can't be too nice to your former lover or you'll look like he or she is getting special treatment, and you can't be too harsh or you'll look like you're taking vengeance for the failed relationship. It's probably impossible to get it just right. You cannot win.

Them

Romance between employees is a bit easier to handle. Usually, coworkers aren't threatened and they don't behave badly. In fact, they may applaud it and wish the couple well. However, after a while the romantic couple may come to be perceived as forming a bloc, in that they help each other do their jobs and vote similarly on issues that are settled by votes. Coworkers are apt to be upset by this, reasoning that this gives them an unfair advantage, an advantage not available to others in the group.

Even if coworkers condone the romance, they usually don't cope well if it breaks up—particularly if the breakup is messy. Having two hostile former lovers working in the same unit is seldom very pleasant. Coworkers tend to take sides, with the result that the unit becomes polarized and new conflicts break out. The situation is ugly and the solution is likely to be uglier. Common sense says that the warring couple should be separated, but do you transfer one or both? If one, which one? If you really must have the skills that one of them possesses and you move the other one, you clearly have problems of a different sort, perhaps a lawsuit.

The moral of this sad tale is to avoid workplace romances if you possibly can and discourage them among your subordinates. If you fail in this, at least talk with the involved parties as soon as possible and set out some rules about how you are going to handle things while the romance is hot, and what you will do if it turns cold. (Most people do not believe romance will cool when it's still new.) You may meet some resistance to having this talk, but you have to do it anyway. It is best to learn to deal with workplace romance, because there will be others after this one. Even when people know it's best not to get romantically involved with their coworkers, it happens. As the novelist John Steinbeck observed, "In the combat between wisdom and feeling, wisdom never wins."

"Crushes"

In the course of working together employees often develop unreciprocated feelings for another a coworker. These "crushes" usually are relatively benign, but when they persist and grow, even after encountering discouragement, they may cross the line into harassment. Some people seem to believe that "no" means "keep trying, and you'll win my heart," but being pestered and harassed never caused anyone to fall in love. Even if the unwanted attention does not qualify legally as harassment, if it makes its recipient uncomfortable or impairs performance, you must step in. In most cases, merely telling the would-be lover to back off is sufficient. Point out that what he or she is doing is alienating the recipient and causing trouble for the unit. Make clear the possible consequences of continuing the unwanted attention and work with the person on a specific plan for change. The plan should focus on immediately stopping the behavior that is causing trouble as well as ways of staying away from the recipient of the unwanted attention: moving to a new workspace, eating lunch at a different time, or even transferring to a different unit. The person shouldn't be treated like a criminal or a sexual predator; after all, the behavior has been motivated by affection and may not have seemed as extreme to that person as it seemed to its recipient. A little sympathy on your part is in order, but not so much that it looks like an endorsement of the behavior or the futile affection that fuels it.

Employees also develop crushes on their managers. Within reason, fond feelings are fine; everybody likes to be liked, even managers. However, fondness becomes awkward if the employee lets it grow into a crush. I have seen cases in which the employee hinted, rather explicitly, to coworkers that the fondness was reciprocated, suggesting a closer relationship between themselves and their manager than actually existed. Usually the coworkers saw the exaggeration for what it was and ignored it or teased the person. Sometimes, however, they believe the falsehood and become very concerned about the special status the supposed relationship gave the person.

Being the object of an employee's crush can be quite unpleasant. You want to discourage the attention, but you don't want to hurt the person's feelings. Moreover, if the person hasn't actually made any obvious overtures, if you just suspect that he or she has a crush on you, it is difficult to know how to cool things off. You can't very well discourage the person or say that you do not reciprocate their feelings if they haven't done or said anything definite. If you try to be forthright and put your cards on the table, he or she is likely to deny having a crush, leaving you looking like a fool. It probably is best to ignore the early signs of a crush, making very sure you don't encourage it in any way. Then, if it doesn't go away, take the first overt sign as an opportunity to make it clear that you do not regard the person as anything other than a valued member of your unit. Don't be cruel, but be firm and clear.

Gifts

Sometimes, fondness, admiration, gratitude, or a desire to impress will lead an employee to give gifts to the manager. It is reasonable for small gifts to be given on special occasions, such as the holidays or your birthday, but employees sometimes overdo it. Gift giving in the workplace is a touchy issue;

people want to show their good feelings toward their manager, but they often don't have a proper sense of proportion. On the manager's side, receiving gifts is nice, but, again, it has to be kept in proportion.

It really is difficult to handle gifts tactfully when there is one sitting on the table in front of you. Do you refuse it and insult the giver? Do you accept it and run the risk of the giver expecting some sort of reciprocity—or having others think you might reciprocate through favored treatment? If you accept a gift from one employee, does it mean you expect gifts from the others? What if they try to outdo each other? It really can create a nightmare if you don't nip it in the bud. By this I mean you have to set up rules early on, so the problem simply doesn't arise; a policy on gifts should be part of the unit's behavioral code, which will be discussed in conjunction with behavioral and performance standards in the following chapter.

Summary

To ensure mastery of the material in this chapter, summarize it for yourself by filling in this topic outline.

I. Drama and Trauma _____

_____

II. Fear _____

_____

III. Anger_____

_____

    A. You_____

_____

        1. Explosive and Strategic Anger _____

_____

    B. Them _____

_____

    C. Explanations and Apologies _____

_____

    D. Hatred and Violence _____

_____

IV. Stress _____

_____

    A. You_____

_____

    B. Them _____

_____

V. Grief

_____

    A. You_____

_____

    B. Them _____

_____

VI. Lust and Love _____

_____

    A. You_____

_____

    B. Them _____

_____

    C. "Crushes"_____

_____

    D. Gifts

_____

Exercises

1. Return to your three managers and ask them questions about their experiences with emotions in the workplace, the causes and the effects. Also ask about their organizations' policies about romantic attachments between management and employees and between employees.

2. Write an essay outlining your views on managing employees, incorporating what you have learned from the text and what you learned in your interviews.

3. Add your essay to your notebook.

Sources and Further Reading

Gutek, B.A. (2002). Sexual harassment. *Encyclopedia of the social sciences, Vol. 4.6,* article 68. United Kingdom: Elsevier.

Kubler-Ross, E. (1997). *On death and dying.* New York: Simon & Schuster.

Lazare, A. (2004). *On apology.* New York: Oxford University Press.

Lazarus, R. (1991). Psychological stress in the workplace. *Journal of Social Behavior and Personality, 6,* 1–13.

Oatley, K. (1999). Why fiction may be twice as true as fact: Fiction as cognitive and emotional simulation. *Review of General Psychology, 3,* 101–117.

Oatley, K., & Jenkins, J.M. (1996). *Understanding emotions.* Cambridge, MA: Blackwell.

Steinbeck, J. (1976). *King Arthur.* New York: McGraw-Hill.

Tilly, C. (2006). *Why?* Princeton, NJ: Princeton University Press.

Wispe, L. (1986). The distinction between sympathy and empathy: To call forth a concept, a word is needed. *Journal of Personality and Social Psychology, 50,* 314–321.

——5————

Setting Standards

Good managers commit to translating their expectations about how employees should behave into clear performance standards.

In Chapters 3 and 4 we discussed the nature of workplace expectations and the emotions people experience when their expectations are violated. Recall that there are two kinds of expectations: expectations about what ideally should happen and expectations about what actually might happen. In this chapter we will focus on expectations about what should happen, specifically, your expectations about what your employees should do. When translated into precise requirements for an individual employee, your "should" expectations become standards against which his or her workplace behavior and job performance can be evaluated.

Communicating Standards

A major part of every manager's job is to convey to employees what is expected of them, that is, behavior and performance standards. In a moment we will discuss just what these standards might look like, but first let us focus on how to communicate them.

The goal is to establish clear standards that reflect your expectations and to communicate them in a way that ensures that employees understand and comply with them. This requires you to:

- Figure out precisely what you expect; you can't set standards if you don't know what you want.
- Select a method of communicating the standards and use it as effectively as possible.

- Check to make sure that the standards you thought you communicated are the same as the standards they thought they received. If there is a discrepancy, correct it and check again.
- Check periodically to see if their understanding continues to coincide with yours to prevent "slippage" or "backsliding." If it has occurred, correct it and check again.
- Adjust your expectations and your standards as events progress to keep them up to date.
- Communicate the adjustments to your employees and then check to see if they have adjusted their understanding accordingly.

The biggest part of setting standards is figuring out what they should be. It is insufficient to tell people to be nice or try hard or cooperate—all of these words mean different things to different people and even those meanings change as circumstances change. True, you can assume a certain degree of commonly shared meaning in the words you use, but if you are trying to establish standards that employees are expected to meet, you must be precise. To be precise, you have to sit down and think through just what is to be accomplished and what standards are required to ensure its accomplishment. Anything not contributing to that goal is irrelevant and you oughtn't be setting standards for it.

The best way to begin this exercise is to figure out what you and your boss expect of your unit. Then, working backward from there, determine what each employee's contribution to that should be and the tasks that he or she performs to make that contribution. At this point you are ready to consider what your expectation is for each task in that employee's contribution.

Having decided on the expectations for an employee, you must decide how to communicate them to him or her. Usually this is done by specifying the expectations in writing and then discussing them in person. Because employees already may be engaged in the tasks in question, they may think that they already know what you expect. If it's true, that's great. But, if it isn't, you have to know it and make sure they update their understanding. Whether the task is familiar or unfamiliar, you have to make your expectations clear, and then you have to make sure that their understanding of your expectations is accurate—misalignment will lead to difficulties when you're unhappy and they don't know why. Failure to have a clear, mutual understanding of what is expected is the greatest source of performance-related conflict between managers and employees.

Sometimes it's useful to have employees repeat back to you what they think your expectations are, as a way of checking their understanding. However, if you've given them your expectations in writing, as well as in face-to-face discussion, you're liable to get your own words back without any real indication of whether they were understood or not. The best way of telling if you and your employees have aligned expectations is by looking at the output of their work. If it pretty much meets your expectations, alignment is close enough and you should provide feedback so they'll know to continue doing things the way they are. If their work doesn't meet your expectations, you must provide feedback so they can change what they're doing—after all, they are using their understanding of your expectations to monitor the quality of their own work. Presuming they want to meet your expectations, they need to know whether they are succeeding or not.

Feedback has to be detailed. Just telling employees that they're falling short of your expectations does not constitute feedback, because it provides no information about how to improve. It simply says, "Don't continue doing what you're doing," which isn't very helpful—what do you do instead? (I knew a football coach who simply swore at his players when they made mistakes and then wondered why they didn't improve.) To be useful, feedback must be detailed and keyed to your performance standards: "Here you fall short and there you exceed the mark." The goal is to help employees more closely align their understanding of what is wanted with your actual expectations.

Work output continues to be the best test of the alignment of expectations long after you've set the standards. If output begins to fall short of what you expect, you know something is wrong. In subsequent chapters, we'll discuss many of the things that could be wrong, but one of the first things you should suspect is "slippage" or "backsliding" toward the standards that existed before you set the current ones. Old habits die hard, and employees sometimes, often without noticing, will lapse into doing things the way they used to do them rather than the way you've come to expect. This is common and normal, so don't get upset. When it happens, simply refresh their understanding of the current expectations.

Finally, employees aren't the only ones who have to modify their expectations—you do too. As a plan is implemented and its effects are felt, tasks must be modified to fit the new circumstances. In addition, the unit's operating environment changes over time, often as a result of changes in the organization's own operating environment and its strategy for dealing with those changes. In both cases, expectations for each employee's performance must be fine-tuned to accommodate those external changes. And changes in your expectations must be communicated to your employees, checks made on their understanding, feedback given, and so on back through the cycle.

It is impossible to overemphasize the importance of successful communication of expectations and useful feedback about how well they are being met. One of the most frequent complaints about managers is that they aren't clear about what they want and they don't give adequate feedback about whether they're getting it. Employees feel like they're sailing a boat through a thick fog, relying on hope and faith that they are headed in the right direction.

Because employees expect you to know what you expect of them and expect you to tell them if they're meeting your expectations, they feel threatened when you don't do it—you might suddenly decide they're performing poorly and punish them. Threat, as we've seen, arouses anxiety, which, if it's bad enough, can prompt a search for another job. If this happens, it is because you failed to do your job. You will have lost someone who is responsible enough to become anxious about doing his or her job well—exactly the kind of person you want to retain.

Setting Standards

We'll begin by looking at the standards you want to set for participation in the organization and unit in general, and then we'll look at setting standards for specific jobs and specific tasks.

General Standards

Every organization, and every unit, has both a culture, which we have already discussed (Chapters 2 and 3), and a climate—a workplace atmosphere that, at its best, encourages participation, cooperation, information sharing, and willingness to do things that are needed but aren't part of one's job description. Climate reflects the degree to which employees feel committed to the organization and unit, and their resulting motivation to create a congenial and effective work environment. On top of that, it reflects the degree to which employees actually know how to conduct themselves in order to create such a workplace. In short, climate is determined by both motivation and knowledge as well as by commitment and conduct.

Presuming that you want to achieve a climate that supports a congenial, effective work environment, where people are upbeat and decent to one another, here is how you go about setting the standards that will promote it.

Commitment

The first key to getting the climate you want is to foster commitment to the organization and to the unit. Research shows that most people are already positively disposed toward organizations when they seek employment. They often live in the same community and know the organization by reputation; they often have friends who already work there. Moreover, they probably have rehearsed scenarios in their minds about what it will be like to work there, so they have expectations before they even arrive.

The first few days on the job can slow or hasten the development of commitment. If you simply throw new employees into their jobs and let them fend for themselves, trusting that they'll meet people and learn the culture, you're going to make it take longer for them to commit. Surely you can remember being the New Kid—the first days at a new school or at camp or at a new job. You felt awkward and alone; it took a while to feel part of the group and even longer to feel committed to the group.

This period of awkwardness can be shortened. All it takes is two people to help the new employee settle in. One is the administrative Go-To Guy, perhaps an administrative assistant or the office manager—someone who can help with getting keys to the building, order office supplies, arrange for computer access, obtain a parking permit, and so on. The other is a colleague who can introduce the new employee to his or her coworkers and give tips about the local social mores. For example, do you leave your plates on the cafeteria tray while you eat, or do you put them on the table and set the tray aside? What do you do with the dirty dishes—leave them or take them somewhere? Understanding these kinds of things may seem trivial, but knowing them helps the new employee settle in more quickly and feel more comfortable.

This second person should be selected carefully. You don't want to put a new employee in the hands of someone who hates his job and dislikes all his coworkers. His idea of helping a new employee settle in might start with lurid tails about everyone in the place, followed by a litany of complaints about all the managers. It probably would take a while for the new employee to overcome the negative impression this introduction would create, and imagine what it would do the new employees' budding feelings of commitment if all of their new coworkers and managers stand accused of villainy.

As the employee settles into his or her job and becomes familiar with the organization and the unit, the initial impression is augmented by how he or she is treated. To a great extent this depends on his or her expectations: Someone who expects work to be interesting and challenging will become more committed if the job meets those expectations. Someone who wants responsibility will become more committed if you give it to them. Someone who is ambitious for advancement will become more committed if opportunities exist. Someone who merely wants to do a day's work for a day's pay and then go home may never be highly committed, but whatever commitment may develop depends on the extent to which the employee's expectations are met.

Of course, employees have private lives, and their friends and family exert an influence on the level of commitment they develop. I once tried to work with a utility company whose employees were so ashamed of its mismanagement, and so tired of their friends' lame jokes, that most of them wanted to quit. But, times were hard and they couldn't find other jobs. So, they simply stopped telling anyone where they worked. That isn't commitment.

If the employee's spouse is unhappy with his or her work schedule or the town or the schools or has conflicting career demands, the employee can't become very committed because he or she may have to leave for a job somewhere else. Some companies make a point of including spouses in their efforts to build employee commitment, with varying degrees of success. The pressures on two-career families and the availability of opportunities elsewhere are major causes of employees' reluctance to commit to their employing organization, and there isn't much you can do about it. If you really want to retain an employee, the best you can do is to make his or her job as desirable as you reasonably can and just hope it's enough.

Evidence suggests that the longer employees stay with an organization, the more committed they become. Of course, this is a chicken-and-the-egg situation; you don't know which comes first, commitment or longevity. Perhaps what happens is that long-time employees develop a big investment in friendships, skills, and knowledge about the organization. Starting over somewhere else may seem daunting; it is easier to commit to this organization.

Research isn't clear about the effects of commitment on job performance, although it is clear that commitment reduces willingness to leave and increases willingness to do the things that produce a good climate. From your point of view, this is good news—you can motivate good job performance in other ways. What you want at this general level is to foster a good climate—willingness to participate, cooperate, share information, and do things that go beyond the narrow job boundaries.

Setting Commitment Standards. Commitment appears to follow a predictable path of development. It is built on the positive expectations new employees bring with them. It is enhanced by their proper introduction to their colleagues, the culture, and their jobs. And it grows as the employee grows within the organization, unit, and job.

But its development can be accelerated and focused if employees know precisely why you expect them to commit and what that means in terms of how they behave. You should explain this during a face-to-face meeting when they first arrive, making it clear that you expect commitment and detailing the behaviors this entails, which are, in fact, the actual standards. Explain that the atmosphere or climate or community, or whatever you want to call it, depends on everyone pitching in, on everyone fostering positive attitudes, on everyone working together and going the extra mile. Anything short of these standards makes working here less agreeable and therefore makes it harder to get the job done, meet the unit's goals, and move the organization forward. Et cetera, et cetera, et cetera—you get the idea; I don't have to write your speech for you.

Setting explicit commitment standards in this way is far more effective than simply relying on their natural development over time. True, some folks will interpret your talk as an invitation to fake it, behaving as though they are committed even though they aren't, but so what? It's the behavior you want, not their hearts and souls. Most employees are inclined to become committed anyway, so your words merely will highlight for them the things they probably would end up doing anyway—they'll just do it sooner. Moreover, even the fakers will be convinced after a while—we know that people are likely to become convinced when they publicly behave as though they already are convinced.

Things are a little harder if you're taking over a unit with disgruntled employees who have either lost their commitment or never developed it in the first place. These folks may have been abused by the organization in the past, and they are leery of committing because they fear being abused again. The only way to win them over is to consistently exceed their expectations (which isn't difficult because they aren't all that high to start with). They can be brought around if you're patient—and they especially profit from your candid talk about your standards for commitment. They may have to fake it for a while, until you prove to them that it is worthwhile to commit, but, again, fake good behavior is almost as good as real good behavior.

As with any standards you set, you have to check from time to time to make sure your commitment standards are being met. The proof is in how people behave—cooperation, going the extra mile, and all that. If an employee hoards information, they aren't meeting the standard. If they do their job and nothing more, they aren't committed.

Another way of checking on commitment is to listen to how employees talk about themselves, their colleagues, and the organization or unit. A few years ago, I was shown around a manufacturing plant by a woman who had only recently been hired. She kept referring to herself as "I" or "me" and everyone else as "they." The plant was very nice; "they" had a day-care center, a gym, a beautiful cafeteria, and the work areas were well lighted and comfortable. Two years later, I was shown around again by the same woman, but this time everything was "we" and "our." She had gone from being an outsider to being an insider. (Whoever assigned her the task of showing visitors around did the right thing; I suspect that by showing the organization to its best advantage to visitors, she quickly convinced herself.) On the second visit she spent as much time telling me how much she loved her job and the organization as she did showing me the newest additions to the plant.

Conduct

Setting standards that promote commitment is the first step in achieving a desirable organizational and unit climate; the second step is setting standards that ensure good conduct. In fact, commitment is the foundation for good conduct because committed employees are motivated to behave in ways that are beneficial to the organization. Standards of conduct simply help them do what they are inclined to do anyway. But, if commitment is low or wavers, or if employees find themselves in situations in which it isn't clear what would benefit the organization, they need guidance. Standards of conduct provide that guidance and help prevent both intentional and inadvertent misbehavior.

Recall that people misbehave for four reasons:

- They genuinely don't know the right thing to do.
- They know the right thing to do, but they don't know when to do it.
- They know what to do and when, but after the first slip, slipping again gets easier and easier.
- They know what to do and when, but the benefits of misbehaving exceed the costs.

To remedy this, many organizations have adopted detailed codes of ethics that define standards for what should be done in "dangerous situations" that employees are apt to encounter. In addition, the codes make clear the consequences employees can expect if they behave in other than the prescribed manner in those situations, consequences designed to make the inevitable cost of misbehaving exceed the possible benefits. Thus, the code addresses all four reasons for misbehavior: It tells employees how to behave, it tells them when to behave that way, and it tells them that the cost of misbehaving is greater than the benefits, thus discouraging the first slip.

Because these codes often include things other than truly ethical issues, such as legal requirements and civil behavior, the name "code of ethics" seems both too grand and not quite accurate. Moreover, ethics commonly refers both to moral issues and to professional customs and conventions (as in "professional ethics"). Recognizing this, some organizations call their code a code of conduct, because it specifies exactly what should be done without reference to morals or customs; it simply presents the rules for behavior that best furthers the organization's interests. We will use this latter term, code of conduct.

Setting Conduct Standards. Units often augment the organization's rather broadly inclusive code of ethics or code of conduct with more specific codes in order to set very clear standards for their employees' conduct. A unit's code should dovetail with the organization's, but it should focus on standards that are particularly relevant to the unit's employees or that are not sufficiently spelled out in the organization's more general code of ethics. Because standards are useless if there are no penalties for failing to meet them, the unit's code must describe the consequences of violating its rules, as well as describing the unit's appeal process. Remember, the point of having a code is to help employees know precisely what is expected of them in situations in which their interests and the organization's interests diverge—as well as the penalties for making the wrong choice.

Constructing a code of conduct is a big job. Because each organization and unit is unique, I doubt you'll find anything out there that you can adopt as is—you'll have to construct your own. A good place to begin is with your own organization's code, seeing how the generalities of that code can be made specific to your unit and building from there. At the very least, your code should include some of the same issues as the organization's code, but specifically tailored to situations your employees encounter.

Another source is the Center for the Study of Ethics in the Professions at the Illinois Institute of Technology, which has compiled a large collection of codes of ethics and codes of conduct, some of which are for small organizations, and may be approximate models for your unit's code. Examples can be found at http://ethics.iit.edu/codes/index.html. This site also has links to articles that may be helpful in writing a code of conduct, the main points of which are in Box 5.1. Examples of codes from business, government, and educational institutions can be found at www.codesofconduct.org.

Unless serious thought is put into them, codes can be useless or even worse than useless. Vague endorsements of goodness and virtue, without any concrete instructions about how they are to be achieved, are a mere statement of sentiment rather than a code. Lists of rules without any rationale for them require a rule for every possible situation; rationale allows employees to infer the general idea behind a rule so it can be applied to situations the rule maker didn't anticipate. People need to know why they should conduct themselves in one way or another as much as they need to know how to conduct themselves and when to do so.

If your organization or unit has an employee handbook, and it should, it may prove convenient to append your code of conduct to it, especially because both documents should be given to new employees upon arrival. Many organizations have handbooks, but most of them are badly out of date; expired policies are never deleted, and new ones are simply pages stuffed into the back cover. Handbooks, and codes, must be updated periodically and reissued to employees—with changes being reviewed at a meeting so everyone is up to date about organizational and unit policies and about how they are expected to conduct themselves.

Box 5.1

Guidelines for Writing a Code of Conduct

Getting Started

✓ Introduce the idea of a code of conduct in a general meeting of your unit, arguing for it as a way of ensuring everyone knows the rules, particularly as a way of bringing new employees up to speed quickly.

✓ Elect a committee unless the unit is small enough for everyone to participate (ten is roughly the upper limit).

✓ Meet to review examples of codes you have downloaded from the Web sites cited in the text. Remember, the code of conduct will constitute the unit's rules and regulations, so its prohibitions must be very specific to what happens, or might happen, in the unit and its requirements must be relevant to the tasks performed in the unit. Requiring employees to respect the flag and be loyal to the government isn't appropriate unless it is necessary for the unit's work.

Drafting the Code

✓ Appoint a committee member to be the "scribe," to summarize discussions in writing and to write a draft of the code based on what is discussed. He or she should be advised to keep it short and to avoid legal jargon, convoluted sentences, and empty generalities. Something cannot be prohibited or required if nobody knows precisely what it is, so things have to be very concrete.

✓ After a draft has been produced, the committee should review and revise it. Then a draft version should be submitted to everyone in the unit for comments. Not all comments will be valuable, but listen to them anyway. Sometimes the vague misgivings that prompt comments are as important as more clearly articulated arguments.

✓ The draft version should be revised in light of the comments and a final version sent to all employees.

Things to Keep in Mind

✓ Focus on "dangerous situations" and the prohibited or required conduct in these situations. Situations are dangerous when the unit's interests are unclear or when one's own interests do not coincide with those of the unit. In the absence of the code, employees guess about the unit's interests and must choose between their own interests and those of the unit. The code tells them what the unit's interests are and what the right choice is, as well as the penalty for making the wrong choice.

Structure the Code

✓ Preamble, which describes what the code is intended to accomplish.
✓ Statement of the values that underlie the rules that are included in the code and that provide the why for the rules.
✓ The body, which contains the actual rules, in numbered categories organized in an outline; the goal is easy reference.
✓ Similar dangerous situations should be grouped in each category under appropriate headings, and the order of the topics should reflect, roughly, their importance. Legal issues should have references to appropriate laws and/or the organization's policy statements and code of ethics.
✓ Examples help clarify definitions and further explain why each rule is necessary, but be careful that they don't give the appearance that the rules apply more narrowly than is intended.
✓ Penalties should be outlined as clearly as possible. When specificity is difficult, at least make it clear that penalties can be imposed and by whom, otherwise the rules have no teeth.
✓ Describe the process by which penalties will be imposed.
✓ Describe the appeal procedure.
✓ Finally, construct an index so people can find relevant topics easily. If the items in your index are discussed in many different places in the code, you may want to take another look at the code's organization; if topic coverage is fragmented and spread all over the place, your code isn't likely to be coherent or user-friendly.

Because you want to write a code of conduct rather than a penal code, you have to be careful about how you incorporate penalties into your written document. The code is supposed to be helpful, not intimidating, although it has to be made clear that misconduct will have negative consequences. One way of being complete without being too heavy-handed is to have a section at the end of the code in which the possible range of penalties is described (get help from your human resources office and/or lawyer on this). Then you can add a symbol at the end of the description of each standard that refers to the listed penalty that its violation will incur.

Writing the unit's code of conduct is only half the job. The other half is getting your employees to read it and abide by it. The best way to ensure this is to have them help write it. They're likely to think of things you won't, and their participation guarantees that they will be familiar with its contents. You have to be in control, however, or everything but the kitchen sink will end up in it. If it gets too cumbersome, new people coming into the unit will never read it and eventually you'll end up right back where you were before you wrote it.

Of course, having a code doesn't guarantee that your employees' conduct will meet its standards. There are three reasons this can happen:

- The penalties are less than the benefits of violating the code.
- The penalties are sufficient, but employees don't believe they will be imposed.
- The culture condones the transgression and either protects the transgressor from punishment or celebrates him or her as a victim or a hero—or both.

First, if the promised punishment is minor in comparison to the anticipated benefits of misbehavior, simple cost-benefit logic works against adhering to the code.

Second, if you are lax about imposing promised punishments or if they are so disproportionately severe that you are disinclined to impose them, they might as well not exist—which means that the code might as well not exist.

Third, you can construct the fanciest code in the world, but if the organization's or unit's culture tacitly gives permission to behave in some other way, it can make the code just so many empty words. Imposed penalties will appear to coworkers as unjust, and the errant employee will be seen as a victim or hero, which makes you the villain. On the other hand, conflict between the code and the culture isn't wholly bad news because it highlights where the organization's and unit's cultures need to be changed, which brings us back to the discussion in Chapter 2 about the importance of culture and about how to change cultures that foster the wrong behavior.

Specific Standards

Standards for commitment and conduct are general in that they are not job or task specific; they are broadly the same for all employees. They are designed to encourage employees to be good citizens of the organization and unit. These standards produce the foundations for good job performance and successful task accomplishment, but they are not themselves useful standards for either. Moreover, in contrast to commitment and conduct standards, job and task standards last only as long as the job exists or until the task is done.

Job Standards

Well-written job descriptions are a rarity, but the good ones explain precisely what the job's duties and responsibilities are, and explain the standards for these duties and responsibilities in terms that will be used for performance evaluations.

In some cases, job descriptions are not written down; the manager explains in person. This isn't a good idea, but it is more common than it should be. For example, when a new professor is hired, their manager (department head) usually assumes that they know what is involved in being a professor. Then he or she may sit down with them and explain that the new job consists of teaching, research, and service, and that annual evaluations will consist of performance scores for each of these three areas. The overall performance score will be a weighted sum of the three area scores, where the weights vary from one employee to another depending on programmatic needs. Suppose the department needs a new professor to focus on teaching, while still engaging in scholarly work and performing necessary service to students and the community; the weights might be 60 percent for teaching, 15 percent for research, and 25 percent for service. From this conversation with the department head, the new professor can conclude that:

- The job has three areas of responsibility.
- The standards for performance emphasize teaching, followed by service to students and the community, followed by scholarly research.
- Investment of time and energy should reflect the standards' emphasis; doing lots of research, no matter how valuable, is unlikely to compensate for poor or indifferent teaching or a second-rate service record. Too, great teaching probably can't wholly compensate for poor service and no scholarly research. The professor has to meet or exceed the standards in all three areas to get high overall performance evaluations and whatever rewards those evaluations bring.

But these face-to-face discussions often fail to make the standards clear. I have seen too many new professors fail to understand them—largely because the specific standard for each of the three areas isn't always clearly specified and because there frequently is no written document to consult. Thinking they understand what's expected of them, they often drift into expecting that truly outstanding performance in just one area (usually the one they enjoy most) relieves them of responsibility for the other two. If students flock to their classes, that ought to be good enough. If they pull in lots of grants and publish lots of papers, it's not important that their courses induce comas. If they serve on tons of committees and get heavily involved in faculty governance, then everything will be fine. They're shocked when their expectations prove to be wrong, when their evaluations in the two neglected areas scuttle their evaluation in the area upon which they've concentrated. As a result, their contract isn't renewed.

The only way to keep employees from misunderstanding or distorting job standards is to be very clear about the standards, to write them down, and to check that they understand them. One way to check is to ask them, and the other is to keep an eye on their performance and give ample and timely feedback about how they're doing. If there is a significant discrepancy between what they tell you and the standards, or between their performance and the standards, you have to help them understand the problem. You can't just wait until the axe falls; it isn't fair. (I must admit, however, that even with clear feedback, some employees never understand that they are failing. I have had more than one young professor tell me flatly that I was wrong when I tried to warn them about neglecting one or another of the three areas. And then I watched sadly as they convinced themselves that the organization had betrayed them when their poor evaluations led to dismissal.)

Task Standards

In theory, you have to supply employees with new standards each time they are assigned a new task. In fact, however, experienced employees doing tasks that are roughly similar from one time to the next soon learn what the task standards are—you only need to monitor the quality of their work to make sure they adhere to the standards.

Task standards usually address the goal of the task as well as how it is to be reached. Research shows that clear, specific, and challenging goals lead to the highest levels of performance—particularly if the method of reaching the goals is fairly clear. Merely telling the employee to do his or her best is too vague and doesn't produce a particularly high level of engagement in the task.

Task standards also must address the priority of the task, including the rationale for pursuing the goal, so the employee knows whether the task should displace other tasks on which he or she is already working. Priority helps the employee determine how much attention to focus on the task, the level of physical and mental effort to devote to it, and the persistence it deserves. Good performance is more about greater understanding than about greater effort because it allows employees to "work smart," adjusting what they are doing to fit the circumstances rather than blindly following a set of instructions that may not, in fact, turn out to be the best way to achieve the desired ends.

Challenging goals, by definition, are not easily achieved. They require committed effort, which arises from the belief that the goal is worthwhile and achievable if you make the effort. Your employees will be more inclined to commit to the task if it is assigned by someone they respect (hopefully, you) who promises (and delivers) continued support throughout the task. Commitment can be increased even further if, for some reason, employees state publicly that they are engaged in the task, that they understand and value the goal, and that they are determined to reach it. (It used to be thought that commitment to goal attainment was enhanced by employee participation in setting the goal, but recent research disputes this—although there apparently is no evidence that participation hurts performance.)

Task standards go beyond goal setting and commitment. In addition, you must provide reasonably specific sub-goals, also called "mileposts," and deadlines for their achievement. Tasks usually build over time, with later efforts using the results of earlier efforts to ultimately bring about successful completion of the task. The output of these various stages of the effort are the sub-goals that must be accomplished before moving on. By identifying particularly notable sub-goals and specifying a time by which they should be accomplished, you set standards against which progress can be measured. Deadline failures should set off alarms—the task is progressing too slowly, or it is off course completely, or, sometimes, things may be going too quickly. Because the results of any task usually must be integrated with the results of other tasks to contribute to the unit's accomplishment of the larger task, the time of completion of each task may be crucial to bringing everything together in an orderly manner. Too slow, or getting off course, clearly is undesirable, but too fast also is bad if things are time-sensitive. For example, if the task is to line up funding for the construction of an addition to your factory, it isn't good to raise the money too far before everything else is ready if you're paying interest on it while you wait.

As with job standards, task standards must be monitored to make sure the employee has not misunderstood or distorted them. Keeping an eye on progress is one way, and the other way is to have employees tell you how things are going and what they think the next few steps should be. A discrepancy between the standards you gave them and what they do or say allows you to bring things back on track. Too, a discrepancy allows you to reexamine the standards themselves; the employee, who is intimately involved in the task and knows its details better than you do, may have found a better way.

Teams

We've been talking as though tasks are always assigned to individual employees. Frequently, of course, they're assigned to teams, so the question arises about how to set standards for teams.

Everything said above about task standards applies to both individuals and to teams; teams need clear, challenging goals and must be told the priority of the task. Every team member has other responsibilities, so each member has to know where the team and its task rank relative to his or her other tasks in order to know which tasks to cut back on.

Note that teams ordinarily are used for one of two kinds of tasks: coming up with ideas or solving problems. Coming up with ideas is a far less structured task than problem solving, if only because nobody knows what the outcome is supposed to look like. A solved problem generally looks solved, but a good idea is sometimes hard to recognize. The difference between these two kinds of tasks is important because teams work differently in pursuing them. Idea generation, or any other ill-defined task, requires a lighter touch than problem solving, or any other well-defined task. The "touch" usually is determined by the approach you take when you assign the task and set task standards, as well as by the approach the team leader takes as he or she herds the group through the task.

If your standards over-constrain a task that properly should be left ill-defined, you'll make it difficult for the team to work on it profitably. For example, if you place too many constraints on a team's efforts to design a logo, you leave no room for creativity. True, you need to specify what the logo is to be used for, and any similar information—perhaps placing some limits on size or other features. But you have to be careful or you will box in the team so much that they'll simply deliver the first thing they come up with that fits the constraints, which may not be the best they can do; it is difficult to be committed to a task that demands creativity if creativity is denied from the start. Similarly, if you place too few constraints on a problem-solving task, leaving everything to the team to decide, you may send them into cycles of indecision as they debate side issues rather than sticking to the task. The point is, your standards must facilitate, not inhibit task accomplishment.

Research shows that the skills of the leader you assign to the group also should fit the task. Some people are "task people," who like to focus on tasks and have an appetite for structure; they shouldn't be asked to lead teams that have ill-defined tasks because they frequently try to structure things, usually prematurely. Other people are "process people," who are particularly comfortable with lack of structure and have an appetite for group deliberation and exploration; they shouldn't be asked to lead teams that have well-defined tasks, because they may get the group bogged down in deliberation and exploration when more mundane problem solving is required. In general, task people do better with well-defined tasks and process people do better with ill-defined tasks, providing in both cases that they have influence over the group members, perhaps by being well liked or being recognized as particularly competent. Of course, some people can vary their leadership style to fit the task and the group, but until you know who these versatile folks are, you'd best not take chances.

It is a good idea to figure out whether you tend toward being a task person or toward being a process person, because you probably will be more comfortable with a team leader who is like you—which isn't always good. I guess I'm a task person, because I'm certainly not a process person. I hate the slow, sloppy stuff of meetings, and I've been told, but I deny it, that I'm not as receptive to everyone having his or her say as I should be. I know I like working with task people because, rightly or wrongly, we get things done. But, I learned long ago that I can't depend on my good feelings about people when selecting team leaders. I have to do it intellectually rather than emotionally, matching the task structure with what seems to me to be the person's style, even though my gut tells me that a task person would do a good job in all circumstances.

This came home to me once again when I assigned leadership of a team to a man whom I had always regarded as the perfect example of a task person—a man I liked and respected. The team was assigned the task of coming up with a creative new plan for revamping a long-established but somewhat threadbare program. I knew the leader should be a process person, but my friend told me he had made contact with his "inner process person"; he was a changed man and was sure he could do the job. I attended a couple of the meetings, and they were awful. His behavior was exactly the opposite of his old directive style, which should have been good, but wasn't. Discussions went on for hours, winding around in circles and covering the same ground repeatedly. As near as I could tell, there had been no progress, and I had decided to disband the committee and try again. The day I was going to announce my decision, the leader unveiled a completely worked out, detailed plan that he had completed, on his own, the day before. The team members were surprised, but they saw a way to avoid more pointless meetings, and, almost without reading it, they endorsed his plan and sent it to me for implementation.

I wasn't happy with this turn of events, because I had wanted to promote buy-in to whatever plan the team came up with by having most of my unit's key players help design it. As it turned out, their buy-in was low despite their having endorsed the plan, because they hadn't helped shape it, but also because they thought they had wasted all that time in the meetings only to have the leader's plan rammed down their throats. I spent months trying to sell the plan throughout the whole organization, largely without the help of the key players from my unit. After that I spent a year implementing it. As it turned out, the plan worked okay, but I always suspected that it would have been better if the committee had worked the way it should have. And, I was reminded, yet again, to use my head, not my emotions, when selecting team leaders.

Your End of the Bargain

Standards work because they lead employees to expect good consequences to follow from commitment, good conduct, and good job and task performance. Their expectation derives from what they see as an implicit bargain between themselves, on the one hand, and you and the organization, on the other hand. Namely, if they live up to their end of the bargain by meeting your standards, you and the organization will live up to yours by making good things happen.

Commitment

Most workers expect that if they commit to the organization, the organization will commit to them. It is precisely because they had come to expect reciprocity that employees feel betrayed and abandoned when they are laid off. Of course, there are organizations for which the expectation of reciprocity is sound, organizations that are committed to their committed employees, but there are many for which it isn't. Even when the expectation is sound, events may prevent the organization from living up to its end of the bargain. When push comes to shove, organizations always look out for their own interests because that is what upper management is paid to do.

Although employees must be dissuaded from excessive faith in reciprocity of commitment, they have to believe that there is at least some or they are unlikely to commit to the organization. This is where you come in. You can't ensure that the organization will reciprocate your employees' commitment, but you can ensure that you will. Therefore, it is your responsibility to step in to fill the gap between the strength of employee commitment and the reciprocal strength of the organization's commitment.

You fill that commitment gap, or at least make it smaller, by committing yourself to championing your unit and your employees to the utmost of your ability. That means that when downsizing comes, you fight to protect your employees. When limited resources are being allocated, you fight for your unit's share. When changes are made, you fight to see that your employees profit from them or are harmed as little as possible. In short, you fill the commitment gap by becoming the defender of your unit and your employees.

Of course, being the defender of your unit and your employees isn't going to fill the commitment gap unless the employees see you doing it and believe you are committed to continue doing it. For them to see you are committed, they have to be part of the struggle, with you as the leader. For them to believe that you are committed, you have to fight every important battle and you have to win more than you lose. Of course, you should choose your battles carefully—don't call out your heavy artillery for petty issues; put most of your energy in the ones you think you can win, but don't let even the little ones go by without some effort. You must demonstrate to everyone in your unit that you are there for them, committed to the unit's and their best interests, and you must demonstrate to everyone outside your unit that you are willing to fight for your unit and your people.

The previous paragraphs sound like a call to constant war, but it seldom actually comes to that. Most "battles" are fairly benign; you merely have to make sure your unit's interests are represented when decisions are being made. Of course, you have to balance your commitment to the organization, of which you are a manager, and your commitment to your employees, whose defender you are. It isn't always easy, but it must be attempted. If you fail, you will be unable to fill the commitment gap and your employees will reasonably conclude that nobody in the organization is looking out for them, so why should they commit to the organization?

If you fail to fill the commitment gap, and if your employees therefore fail to become committed to the organization, they have no reason to follow any code of conduct other than what is dictated by their own sense of responsibility and their fear of being punished—and an uncaring organization doesn't arouse a huge sense of responsibility. Employees whose actions are guided primarily by a desire to avoid punishment are going to become rigid and rule-bound, lacking in initiative and timid about doing anything that isn't covered by the rules, because they have no faith that good intentions will be recognized or well received. This is the exact opposite of employees whose actions are guided by their commitment to the organization and their desire to do things that will benefit the organization.

Rewards

Standards for jobs and tasks lead employees to expect that meeting or exceeding them will result in specific rewards and failure to meet them will result in specific penalties. We'll focus on the rewards in what follows, with just a word or two toward the end about penalties. Chapter 7 will expand on penalties as a feature of problem-solving strategies.

The major reward for meeting or exceeding standards doesn't come from you, it comes from the employee satisfying his or her work ethic. The work ethic is the employee's own personal set of standards for job performance, often higher than the standards you set and largely unrelated to the rewards or penalties you promise. It is what differentiates a competent employee from an irreplaceable employee.

There isn't much you can do to enhance an individual's work ethic—other than providing challenging goals so it really kicks in—but there is a lot you can do to interfere with it. If employees think that their jobs are trivial, purposeless, or dead end, they may suspend their work ethic and do only enough to retain their job until they can find more worthwhile employment. They also will suspend their work ethic if you consistently fail to acknowledge a job well done, discourage initiative, ignore good ideas, or take personal credit for their work.

Formal Rewards

Aside from satisfaction of the work ethic, there are both formal and informal rewards for meeting or exceeding job and task standards. Formal rewards are money, status, and opportunity. Informal rewards are approval and appreciation.

Money. Monetary rewards are valued because they contribute to the improvement of the recipient's life. This goes beyond just pay raises or bonuses, although those are common and highly valued rewards. It also includes things that would cost money if the recipient were to purchase them, for example, a trip for two to Greece or a new car. In addition, it includes things that improve the quality of the recipient's work-life: new equipment for doing one's job better or more conveniently, being assigned more help, or being sent for advanced training. All of these rewards make the recipient's personal or work life better in some way, which, after all, is the purpose of money.

Status. Most of us find public acclaim highly rewarding because it enhances our self-esteem and raises our stature in the eyes of others. Frequently, status rewards are merely symbolic. That is, they have little or no intrinsic worth, but they signal that the recipient has done something that others should honor and might well emulate: the year's top salesman gets a loving cup with his name and achievement engraved on it, the employee of the month gets her picture on the wall, after fifty years of service the retiring maintenance man gets a wooden plaque inscribed with words of thanks. All of these fairly useless trophies are rewarding simply because they let the recipient and everyone else know that he or she has exceeded institutional expectations, that the achievement is valued, and that he or she therefore deserves recognition.

Titles are often equally symbolic. I've known people who were thrilled when they were promoted and given a fancy title even though the pay raise was minimal or even nonexistent. The so-called title inflation that characterizes modern institutions results from the status that titles provide—so janitors become facilities engineers, clerks become sales associates, secretaries become administrative assistants, and banks have more vice presidents than tellers. And the people who already have titles similar to the new, inflated titles now have to have even more inflated titles so they don't lose status. It would be funny if it didn't work so well and it weren't so important to people. I would bet that most people would prefer being rewarded with a nice sounding title than with a small raise. There's a lot more pleasure in "Hey Mom, they've made me a Vice President," than in "Hey Mom, I got a 2 percent raise."

Opportunities. Arguably, this is the most valuable class of rewards. Money is soon spent, status loses its initial zest, but opportunity provides hope for the future. Surveys repeatedly show that employees aspire to new responsibilities, more responsibility, greater ability to influence events, and access to future advancement. In short, most employees want the ability to build a career rather than just fill a job. Therefore, career-building opportunities are extremely rewarding, and most of us will work hard to get them.

You can infer from what has been said that formal rewards are primarily about public communication. They announce to the recipient that he or she has done well, and to keep up the good work. They announce to coworkers that employees who do as the recipient does are valued by the organization, by the unit, and by you, the manager. They announce to people outside the unit that your employees are exemplary, and the unit and its manager deserve some of the reflected glory.

Because formal rewards say far more than Job Well Done, having broader messages for a broader audience, they must be done properly. The procedure by which they are awarded must be clear and credible.

There have to be clear criteria for making awards—which means that you have to be able to measure behavior relative to the pertinent standards in order to tell whose behavior exceeds them most. Imprecise or sloppy measurement makes a mockery of comparing one employee's performance with another's and therefore calls into question the legitimacy of rewarding one person rather than another.

Credibility also requires there to be as little subjectivity as possible in the award procedure, so bias or suspicions of bias don't undermine trust in its integrity. Pity the poor recipient of a reward that is later revealed to be undeserved. The recipient's reputation is tainted, even if he or she is wholly innocent of wrongdoing. The reputation of the person who awarded the reward is tainted. The whole reward process is brought into question, and every previous reward becomes suspect.

Informal Rewards

Most rewards aren't given at ceremonies or announced in letters with embossed letterheads. Most are given informally, face-to-face by the manager to the employee, often merely in passing—in the hallway, in the elevator, or over lunch. They don't bestow money, trophies, or titles, and they usually don't have immediate implications for raises or opportunities. They are simply expressions of approval and appreciation from you to an employee; recognition of a job well done. These informal rewards are nearly indistinguishable from feedback, except that they contain an added element of approval and appreciation. As you can imagine, sincerity is everything; even a hint of insincerity looks like manipulation, which is quite the opposite of rewarding.

Surveys show that employees value feedback/reward of this kind very highly. It both keeps them on track and charges their batteries. When they think they deserve it but don't receive it, they become dissatisfied with their manager, with the organization, and with their jobs: "Nobody ever says thanks!" Considering how easy, inexpensive, and rapid this kind of reward is, you'd think managers would be overflowing with it. But no, they really seem to have difficulty using this effective way of building commitment and providing positive feedback.

The reason is that most managers fail to recognize the importance of day-to-day behaviors that only meet or slightly exceed the standards, not understanding that cumulatively it is these unspectacular successes that make or break the unit. Instead, they focus almost exclusively on failures to meet standards while regarding small successes as simply what is supposed to happen and therefore not deserving of attention. In this they are like so many parents; if their child behaves, they regard it as unremarkable because that is how children are supposed to act, so they pay no attention. But if the child misbehaves, they immediately pay attention in an attempt to discourage future misbehavior. Managers expect their employees to meet or exceed performance standards; that's what they're supposed to do, it's their job. Doing it doesn't even merit comment; but failing to do it requires efforts to keep them from failing again. This obsession with detecting and preventing failure keeps managers from being leaders and turns them into enforcers whose job is to keep employees in line.

If the standards are designed to be challenging, as they should be, meeting them is not commonplace and exceeding them, even a little bit, is worthy of comment. It is in this mid-range of performance, at or near the standard, sometimes exceeding it a little, that informal rewards are at home—the quiet, sincere expression of appreciation, congratulations, and encouragement in passing or when you drop into the employee's office or work station. The accomplishment doesn't demand a formal reward; you don't want to make too much of it. Instead, you want to acknowledge and encourage the employee's effort and attitude, and let them know that you have noticed and that you care enough to say something. This small gesture will mean more than you can

imagine (just think how you feel when your boss does it to you), and it will
send the employee back to work with renewed commitment and energy.

Try to keep informal rewards small; it is tempting to make them bigger if
you've given them to the employee before. I had a boss who somehow got
the idea that something I had done required him to take me to dinner at a
restaurant—just the two of us. I would rather have walked naked through hell.
We had nothing in common but work, and we couldn't converse as equals
about that. As a result, he hardly spoke, and when he did, it was merely to
ask me questions—I felt like I was taking an exam. If that was a reward, I
shudder to think of what punishment might have been.

Penalties

Formal Penalties

Formal penalties are those described in your code of conduct. They are formal
in that they are institutionally condoned and are public, as opposed to informal
penalties that are just between you and the employee. We'll discuss formal
penalties later in the book (Chapter 7), so for the moment we'll simply note
that they consist of disciplining (written reprimands, suspensions, demotions,
pay cuts, fines) and dismissal.

Informal Penalties

Just as a quiet word of approval and appreciation serves as an effective informal
reward, verbal disapproval and verbal reprimands can be effective penalties for
failure to meet standards. The range is from simple feedback with no particular
tone of disapproval or disappointment—simply the facts—to fairly strong
statements that make it clear that you are distressed about the failure to meet
standards. There are, of course, different levels of distress. Telling people they
fell short and that you're disappointed can be very effective (again, think of
how you'd react if your boss said that to you). But, in some cases you want
to make very sure they understand what you're saying. If you say that they
fell short accompanied by a flash of anger, it is likely to have a sizable impact
(but don't waste anger on little things or it will lose its impact).

Of course, your approval or disapproval is effective only in proportion
to how much your employees care what you think. If you lack credibility,
if they don't think you are committed to them or the unit, if you are insin-
cere, if your reaction is disproportional to the failure, if you are seen as
using approval to flatter or disapproval to bully, you might as well forget
it. Your informal rewards will be seen as hollow, and your informal penal-

ties will be seen as meaningless. Unfortunately, if your informal rewards and penalties become ineffective, you must ramp up to formal rewards and penalties, which are more cumbersome and more severe. Formal means just that; you have to go through channels, you have to justify what you do, you have to be willing to take the consequences if others deem your rewards or penalties to be unwarranted or inappropriate. Ultimately, having to rely exclusively on formal rewards and penalties makes you manage by rules and turns you into a rule enforcer. It makes your employees retreat to rule-bound performance, which is rigid and lacking in innovation and creativity. What possible satisfaction can you or your employees derive from working in this kind of situation?

In the following chapter we will examine what happens when standards are not met. Since it isn't always immediately clear what has caused the problem, we will discuss how you go about figuring out the cause. Then in chapter 7 we will discuss what you can do to correct the problem.

Summary

To ensure mastery of the material in this chapter, summarize it for yourself by filling in this topic outline.

I. Translating Expectations into Standards _____

_____

II. Communicating Standards _____

_____

III. Setting Standards _____

_____

    A. General Standards _____

_____

        1. Commitment _____

_____

        2. Conduct _____

_____

    B. Specific Standards _____

_____

1. Job Standards _____

_____

2. Task Standards _____

_____

3. Teams _____

_____

IV. Your End of the Bargain _____

_____

A. Commitment _____

_____

B. Rewards _____

_____

1. Formal Rewards _____

_____

2. Informal Rewards _____

_____

C. Penalties _____

_____

1. Formal Penalties _____

_____

2. Informal Penalties _____

_____

Exercises

1. Return to your three managers and ask them questions about how they figure out what they expect of their employees and how they transform those expectations into standards. What do they do when the standards are not met? What forms of rewards and penalties do they employ?

2. Write an essay outlining your views on managing employees, incorporating what you have learned from the text and what you learned in your interviews.

3. Add your essay to your notebook.

Sources and Further Reading

Locke, E.A. (2000). Motivation, cognition and action: An analysis of studies of task goals and knowledge. *Applied Psychology: An International Review, 49,* 408–429.

Locke, E.A., & Latham, G.P. (2005). Goal setting theory: Theory building by induction. In K.G. Smith & M.A. Hitt (Eds.), *Great minds in management* (pp. 128–150). Oxford: Oxford University Press.

Porter, L.W., Steers, R.M., & Mowday, R.T. (2005). Do employee attitudes towards organizations matter? The study of employee commitment to organizations. In K.G. Smith & M.A. Hitt (Eds.), *Great minds in management* (pp. 171–189). Oxford: Oxford University Press.

Steers, R.M. (1977). Antecedents and consequences of organizational commitment. *Administrative Science Quarterly, 22,* 46–56.

6

Evaluating Problems

Good managers commit to carefully evaluating the problems that arise when their own and their employees' expectations are not met.

In preceding chapters we focused on expectations and standards and how employees, and you, react when they are threatened or violated. In everyday language, a threatened or violated expectation is a problem and the process of preventing or rectifying the violation is problem solving. In this chapter we will examine workplace problems and how to figure out what caused them. In the following chapter (Chapter 7) we will examine how to solve them.

One of the things that troubles employees most is their managers' tendency to "solve" problems before they really understand what's going on. Rushing to judgment too frequently results in employees being blamed for problems they do not cause and application of solutions that do not work. Even when they think they know what the problem is, and what should be done about it, good managers hold off until they are sure. This chapter is about how you make sure you understand performance problems and failures to meet performance standards, so you can apply the appropriate solutions. Of course, you never can be completely sure you understand everything—reaching utter certainty would take too much time and probably be impossible anyway—but you can reduce the chances of being wrong if you take the trouble to seek relevant information and use it wisely. Moreover (and this is a Really Big Thing!), you have to consciously work to avoid biased thinking.

Problems arising from being a manager differ from other problems in your life in two ways. First, problems at work involve failure to meet performance standards, which then makes problems for your unit or the organization that depends on your unit's output. Second, at work the system is designed to make you more clearly accountable for how you go about dealing with problems than is the case in your private life, and your career depends on how well you do it. In your private life you sometimes can finesse problems; for instance, you might just grit your teeth until your child gets through adolescence, or you can move away if your neighbor is intolerable, or you can simply avoid discussing topics upon which you and a friend disagree. This seldom is an option for work-related problems. You can't merely endure, leave, or ignore even minor work-related problems because they are likely to escalate rather than go away. As a consequence, these problems must be resolved before they get out of hand.

Performance problems are in some way the hardest. They usually seem obvious, but they seldom are. In most cases, all you know at first is that performance is off—something is wrong, standards aren't being met. Therefore, your first task is to figure out (evaluate) what is happening; whether a problem actually exists and, if so, how serious it is. If it exists and is serious enough to warrant your intervention, then your second task is to figure out (attribute) what causes it so you can decide how to solve it. Both of these tasks, evaluation and causal attribution, are aimed at establishing a linkage between the events that are making you uneasy and the conditions that are causing those events, because you will solve the problem by breaking that linkage—either by removing the cause or by fixing things so the cause no longer leads to the undesirable effect. Of course, the undesirable effect you are trying to eliminate is failure to meet performance standards, that is, violation of your expectations about what your employees (or you) should do to successfully perform their jobs.

Establishing a linkage between cause and effect in performance problems is difficult because most of your information comes from people who have a vested interest in your conclusion. Even when they try to be objective, they frequently will tell different stories about what the problem is and what causes it. Some stories will be fairly accurate, some won't. Discerning the truth is a challenge because you have no unimpeachable source against which to check the accuracy of what you are told—you only have the stories themselves. Therefore, your task, like that of a detective trying to solve a mystery, is to gather and interpret the stories of everyone involved and use your good sense to discover the thread of truth in them.

Discerning the truth is complicated by the tendency of the people you talk with to focus on people rather than circumstances as the source of the problem. As we will discuss below, performance problems are not always attributable to flaws in the persons most closely associated with the problems; they often are caused by factors that reside in the situation (workspace layout, job design, etc.). Stories that are biased toward attribution of poor performance to persons and their characteristics can be misleading; your job is to see through the confusion and decide whether the problem is properly attributable to person causes, situation causes, or a combination of the two.

Evaluating Performance Problems

Most problems start small and grow until performance is so compromised that they can't be ignored. When they're small, these problems may not be at all obvious—you just feel uneasy, that something isn't right. People are amazingly sensitive to disparities between how things are and how they should be; even when they aren't quite sure what is wrong, they feel vaguely troubled. Even a small disparity between what you see happening and what you expect should happen can set off an alarm in your mind. You should listen to that alarm; it's your early warning system.

The difficulty with disparities is that they merely tell you that something is wrong—not precisely what is wrong, or why. Your job is to figure out exactly what is wrong, and whether it is serious enough to require fixing. Then, if you decide something is wrong and it is serious, you must figure out what is causing the problem. Remember, you're like a detective, looking at clues and trying to construct a story about whether a crime has been committed; how serious is it and why did it happened? Of course, just like in a detective story, the most obvious story often isn't the true story—or at least it isn't the whole story.

You begin by trying to identify the disparity that is making you feel uncomfortable, that is setting off your internal alarm. What is wrong? Some examples of disparities (clues) that may signal the existence of problems:

- Decreased productivity
- Missed deadlines
- Increased absenteeism
- Poor morale
- Lack of teamwork
- Conflict between employees
- Customer or supplier complaints
- Coworker complaints

Each of these, and others like them, could be a sign that something serious is developing—or maybe not. Each sets off your alarm enough to prompt you to look a little more deeply, to figure out if it is a signal that something actually has gone wrong or is merely a temporary glitch that can safely be ignored. This brings us to our first tool for dealing with work-related problems.

First Tool: Ask Questions

You'd be surprised how many managers hate to ask questions, probably because it means coming in contact with the employees who are the apparent source, or the apparent victims, of the problem. This is because most of us hate conflict and we assume that if we ask questions, we are going to end up in some kind of confrontation. Instead, we start weaving theories in our minds to account for why the problem has arisen, but, of course, building theories in the confines of your mind doesn't give you any new information. You need to expand your knowledge, and the fastest, easiest way of doing it is to ask questions. If someone's performance is poor, ask him or her why and, when appropriate, ask coworkers why. If someone is unhappy about a coworker, ask both of them for details—separately.

You don't have to be confrontational when you gather information: you're not in a courtroom conducting a cross-examination and you're not really a detective, so don't act like one. It is my experience that if you are straightforward and low key, open-minded and non-accusatory, things go reasonably well. I've seldom been yelled at and I've never been assaulted.

You don't need to apologize for asking questions; it is your job. But you have to make it clear that you are trying to find out what is going on rather than gathering evidence to support a foregone conclusion—which, after all, is what you're trying to avoid. Nothing will destroy an employee's cooperativeness more quickly than the suspicion that he or she is being accused of something or that you are looking for a scapegoat. The employee will become defensive and angry, both of which complicate your task of getting to the cause of the problem. Your job is to be an unbiased, neutral inquirer—the person who is trying to make sense of everyone's point of view and not a cop out to make an arrest or a lawyer out to get a conviction. Be firm but not tough; toughness and questions don't mix because getting honest answers requires the other person to be in a cooperative frame of mind. Acting tough usually gets a tough reaction and nobody budges.

Fairness and objectivity are always important, but they're crucial when the problem involves conflicts between employees. If a employee complains about a coworker, you must not presume the complaint is valid and demand the coworker explain himself or herself—the person who complained may be the source of the problem, or there may not be a problem at all, just a misunderstanding.

At one time newspaper reporters were advised to structure their news stories around five key words: *What* happened, *when* did it happen, *where* did it happen, *who* was involved, and *why* did it happen? You should follow this advice. Asking questions that address each of these key words, although not necessarily in the order I listed them, allows you to get a good idea about what the person you are questioning thinks happened and why. Using the key words also allows you to have points of comparison among the various stories you hear, helping you detect the common thread.

Knowing what you want to learn (based on the five key words), you can begin meeting with employees to ask questions. For example, if an employee has complained about a coworker, you need to talk to the employee, the co-worker, others who work with the two, perhaps with Human Resources and/or your manager, and maybe with one or two other managers who may have had experience with this kind of situation. Unfortunately, most of us don't know how to ask questions that will yield the kind of unbiased diagnostic information we need. Box 6.1 contains guidelines for asking questions; what to do and what to avoid.

Using the Answers

To complete the first step toward understanding the problem, you must use the answers you have obtained to your questions to determine if there is, in fact, a problem serious enough to warrant your concern.

- Existence of a problem is revealed when a number of employees you talk with agree that it exists.
- Seriousness of a problem is revealed by the degree to which the employees you talk with are concerned about it, either because it is interfering with their own performance or with the smooth operation of the unit, or because the problem causes them significant moral or emotional discomfort.

Existence of a problem does not necessarily oblige you to do anything. Even moderately serious problems are sometimes best left to play themselves out while you simply watch to make sure time is working its cure. On the other hand, if the problem is so serious that the employees you talk to clearly think something should be done, you probably should do something.

Sometimes the problem should be passed along to other people, usually Human Resources, Legal, Security, or all of them. Most jobs have fairly defined boundaries on what kind of problems the manager is responsible for and what should be passed off to others. Problems that involve the law or serious violations of organizational policy should be left to the specialists. After all, your organization's legal unit, security unit, and human resource unit all exist to help you with problems that lie outside the boundaries of your responsibility and expertise.

Box 6.1

Guidelines for Asking Questions

What You Should Do When Asking Questions

✓ Before talking with a potential source of information, clarify in your mind just what it is you want to know—not the answers you want to hear, but the general features of the problem about which you need the employee to furnish information (what, where, when, who, and why).

✓ Meet with each employee individually in a setting that permits frank discussion; group meetings or meetings where other employees can overhear your conversation inhibit honesty and tend to generate a "party line" that provides consistent, but not necessarily accurate, answers to your questions.

✓ Approach the meeting in a businesslike manner; neither too friendly nor too brusque, simply a no-nonsense focus on the problem and the questions you need answered.

✓ Decide ahead of time how confrontational and firm you want to be. Low confrontation might mean meeting in either a neutral workspace, such as a conference room, or in the employee's workspace, with both of you sitting down, your chairs at a 45° angle to each other, while having coffee and speaking in a conversational tone and manner. High confrontation might mean meeting in your workspace, with you standing and the employee sitting, or with the two of you face-to-face across a table, with no refreshments, and with you speaking slightly more loudly and more formally than usual.

✓ Keep your questions simple, making sure that each question is only one question, not multiple questions imbedded in one sentence. Asking complex or confusing questions produces muddled answers.

✓ Limit your questions to the topic at hand and help the employee keep on track, avoiding tangents and irrelevancies.

✓ Give the employee time to think, to remember, to formulate his or her answer rather than rushing him or her or breaking the silence because it makes you feel uncomfortable. Silent intervals are okay; you can wait for an answer.

✓ If you meet in your workspace, keep a box of tissues somewhere across the room. Even what may seem to be innocuous questions can evoke strong emotions. When this happens, get up and walk slowly to the tissues. Take a moment to get the box and walk back across the room. Set the box down near the employee, without comment but as nonjudgmentally as possible. When he or she has pulled himself or herself together, proceed as though nothing much out of the ordinary has happened. This tissue-getting routine serves a number of functions:

- First, it allows you to acknowledge the emotion without having to react to it. A show of sympathy or an attempt to sooth the emotion might derail your inquiry. Even if the employee doesn't mean them to do so, tears often can manipulate you more effectively than shouting. Emotions are to be expected and accepted, but they don't negate the need for the employee to answer your questions.
- Second, it allows a moment for the employee to regain control without your looking on. Most people become embarrassed when they reveal their emotions and some become angry, both at themselves and at you. A moment alone allows them to regain their dignity.
- Third, it provides the employee a tissue with which to wipe away tears and blow his or her nose—it's hard to regain dignity when one's nose is running.

What You Shouldn't Do When Asking Questions

✓ Don't apologize for having to ask questions, this is part of your job.

✓ Don't ask leading questions, that is, questions that themselves suggest an answer—particularly the answer you might want to hear.

✓ Don't let the employee deflect your questions with grievances of his or her own, thereby redirecting the conversation and giving him or her control of it.

✓ Don't get drawn into an argument; simply refuse to be baited into a contest of charges and counter-charges.

✓ Don't trade confidences as a way of encouraging the employee to give more honest, perhaps quite personal, answers. In normal conversation it is common to trade confidences as a way of demonstrating trust and encouraging intimacy. This seldom is appropriate in a business setting and certainly is inappropriate when you are seeking information aimed at helping you do your job properly. Suggesting that you too have engaged in office theft, for example, is not a good way to get an employee to admit knowledge of such goings-on. If nothing else, such revelations preclude you from taking a moral stance if you have to punish someone for similar offenses.

✓ Don't give away your reaction to answers by what you say, the expression on your face, or body language. If the employee you are questioning says something to which you shout, "What?" with a disgusted look on your face and a visible cringe, you probably shouldn't count on any more honest answers. Conversely, if you make it obvious that you like a particular answer, you may lead the employee to slant subsequent answers in ways that will continue to elicit your approval.

✓ Don't finish the meeting by drawing conclusions or making any prom-ises. Merely say that you will think about what the employee has said, together with any other information you obtain, and that you will discuss your conclusions and decisions with him or her at a future time.

✓ Don't forget to get back to each employee you question. The employee deserves to be told in person about the outcome of your information quest, especially if there are consequences that affect him or her.

Second Tool: Causal Analysis

If the first tool, questioning, reveals that there is a problem serious enough to require your attention, the next step is to use what you have learned to figure out what is causing it. Establishing causation can be a tricky proposition because the most immediately apparent cause may not in fact be the actual cause—or not the whole cause.

Attribution Biases

Scientists have done a great deal of research on how people make attribu-tions about the causes of problems. Their major finding is that most of us tend to be biased toward attributing problems to factors residing within the employees involved and biased against attributing the problem to factors residing within the situation in which the problem arises. That is, we tend to think that employees are more in control of things than they actually may be. After all, a great deal of what people do in the course of a day is dictated by the circumstances in which they find themselves.

Let me give you an (embarrassing) personal example: When I was young and inexperienced, I found myself in charge of a mental health clinic that was part of a larger unit that I supervised. The clinic had a staff of thirty clinicians and a receptionist at the front desk. It was brought to my attention that the clinicians had difficulty getting files from the receptionist, that files were not re-filed in a timely manner, that phone messages were not always forwarded, and that clients often had to wait a long time to get checked in. Most of the clinicians' complaints were centered on the receptionist; she wasn't smart enough, fast enough, organized enough, or dedicated enough.

In the course of looking into the clinicians' complaints, I quickly concluded that things were not going well at all. I called the receptionist into my office, told her about the complaints, and asked her what she planned to do about it. She cried for a while, I gave her a tissue, and she assured me that she would try harder. In less than a week, I received more complaints. Concluding that the receptionist simply lacked the capacity to do the job, I fired her.

It wasn't until she was gone that I realized how wrong I had been in attributing the problem to her. When I tried to update her job description so I could hire a replacement, I found that the demands and constraints of the situation were such that one person could not possibly do the job alone. I had to hire two people to replace the receptionist I had fired, which made me feel exceptionally stupid for having attributed the problems to her and having ignored the pressures and constraints of the situation in which she was forced to work. I felt even worse when she got a job at a place where some of my friends worked; they thought she was the most efficient, capable, good-natured receptionist they had ever had, and they were amazed that I had let her get away. To top it all off, every time I saw her, she thanked me for dismissing her because she was so happy in her new job. Although her joy was some consolation, each time she thanked me, I felt even more of a fool.

So, where did I go wrong? Quite simply, I was guilty of jumping to conclusions about the cause of the problem that prompted the clinicians' complaints. I let their opinions color my thinking about what was wrong and what caused it, leading me to assume that I understood the problem when I didn't. This fed right into my all-too-human bias toward attributing the causes of problems to employees (the receptionist's supposed incompetence, etc.), when, in this case, the cause actually lay in the situation (the demands and constraints of a very poorly designed work situation). Finally, mistakenly thinking I understood the cause of the problem when I didn't, I went for the easiest solution—I asked her to shape up, and when she didn't, I fired her.

Self-serving Bias

Before we get to the details of causal analysis, there is another attribution bias you need to know about. Research shows that most of us tend to attribute good outcomes to our own actions and bad outcomes to situational constraints or to others' actions. For the most part, this is a fairly harmless delusion; it serves to protect our self-esteem (Sigmund Freud referred to this as "ego defense"). Without it we might become quite depressed about the sheer magnitude of our own ineptitude. But it ceases to be harmless when it leads us to attribute problem causation to the situation or to employees when, in fact, we are ourselves the cause.

In order to effectively supervise other people, you have to be able to see yourself honestly. After all, you are a major feature of your employees' lives. Problems arising from what they do may well be a result of what you do or of what they think you want them to do. In short, you have to factor yourself and your influence into your attempt to understand problems arising from what they do.

For example, I once supervised a group of six or so office workers. One caused a lot of trouble for my other employees, who quickly let me know that he was an interfering pain in the neck. When I reflected on what was going on, it became clear that I was the major source of the problem. I was favoring him. I thought he was especially able and, without realizing it, I granted him more freedom than I granted the others. Moreover, I usually listened more carefully to his opinions and tended to act on them. Clearly, I was the culprit. Anybody would behave as he did if they were the manager's favorite. So, he got cocky and behaved as though he were a kind of "assistant manager," by criticizing his coworkers' work when I was there and bossing them around when I wasn't. It was only after I backed off, and asked him to back off, that things improved.

Performing a Causal Analysis

Causal analysis, the second tool for understanding problems, is designed to help you use the answers you obtained using the first tool, asking questions, to determine the problem's cause. You begin by considering two Safeguard Questions to make sure the problem isn't just a mistake and to make sure you aren't the cause of the problem. Then you move on to two Diagnostic Questions aimed at helping you overcome your bias toward attributing the causes of problems to employees rather than the situation. Finally, you enter the answers to the Diagnostic Questions into one of the cells in a Diagnostic Table such as in Box 6.2 and consider the Action Implications of your analysis for taking action to solve the problem.

Safeguard Questions

1. Is the problem a result of accident or misunderstanding; was it merely misinterpreted as an employee problem by you or other people?
    • If Yes, do nothing other than repair the damage and clear up misconceptions.
    • If No, go to the next question.
2. Am I the cause of the problem?
    • If Yes, shape up.
    • If No, proceed to the second step in the causal analysis.

Box 6.2
Diagnostic Table for Causal Analyses

		*Reference	
		Specific	General
**Situation	Specific	Cell A This employee in this situation	Cell B This situation
	General	Cell C This employee	Cell D Human nature

Diagnostic Questions

1. Does the problem arise only in *reference to a specific employee or is it more general?
2. Does the problem arise in a specific **situation or is it more general?

Diagnostic Table

• Your answers to these two Diagnostic Questions (*Reference and **Situation) will fall into one of the four cells in the Diagnostic Table in Box 6.2.

Action Implications

1. If your answers fall in Cell A, the cause of the problem lies in the interaction between this particular employee and this particular situation—change either the person or the situation, or both.
2. If the answers fall in Cell B, the cause of the problem probably lies in the situation—change the situation.
3. If the answers fall in Cell C, the cause of the problem probably lies in the employee—change the person.
4. If the answers fall in Cell D, the cause of the problem is undefined because it arises for a variety of employees in a variety of situations—investigate the problem more thoroughly to diagnose the cause(s).

Of course, this causal analysis isn't foolproof, but it helps you think more carefully about the problem and its probable causes.

It Depends Where You're Looking

Establishing causality is tricky. What might be employee-caused from one viewpoint may be situation-caused from another viewpoint. Suppose that you are my manager and you pick up on rumblings from my coworkers about the deteriorating quality and promptness of my work. Because I have always done acceptable work in the past, you decide to look into what is going on before it begins to affect the whole unit's productivity. So, you talk to my coworkers (individually) to find out what they're unhappy about, and then you talk with me. They tell you I've become lazy and irresponsible. I, on the other hand, tell you that I'm trying to do my job, but I'm being driven nuts by noise from the cubical next to mine, noise that continues despite my repeated pleas for quiet. I tell you that even though my neighbor wears earphones, he plays his music so loudly that I simply cannot concentrate, which impairs my ability to deliver good work on time.

Now, is my poor performance caused by employee or situation factors? Certainly, from my viewpoint the cause lies in the situation—the loud music from the next cubical makes it difficult for me to do my work. But, from your viewpoint the whole question shifts: Why is the guy in the next cubical playing music so loudly in spite of pleas to turn it down? Perhaps his behavior is caused by internal factors (maybe he is an inconsiderate jerk or maybe he has listened to loud music for so long that he's hard of hearing and has to have it loud). Or, perhaps it is caused by as-yet-unknown situational factors. Suppose you asked him about the music and he tells you that he plays it loudly because there is a buzz in the air conditioning system that sets his teeth on edge and makes it impossible for him to concentrate on his work. He complained to the maintenance people, but they told him they couldn't hear a buzz and walked away.

Thus, my neighbor's attempt to make sure his own performance is unimpaired, by playing loud music to cover the annoying buzz, ends up impairing my performance. He has, in effect, solved his performance problem by passing it on to me, which isn't very nice but you can see why he might do it. When the problem surfaced in the form of complaints from my coworkers about my performance, the problem was passed on to you, in that you had to find the beginning of the chain of causes and fix it. In this case, fixing the buzz in the air conditioner is good deal easier than trying to fix my presumed laziness and irresponsibility or trying to fix the presumed inconsiderateness or hearing loss of the guy in the next cubical.

This example illustrates the chain of causes that frequently lies behind problems. It is my hunch that about 70 percent of all performance problems can be traced back to situational causes that you can do something about, 20 percent can be traced to employee causes you can do something about, and 10 percent can be traced to either situation or employee causes that are beyond your control. Presuming that my hunch is even roughly correct, these numbers mean that:

Until you learn otherwise, the odds are good that the ultimate cause of a performance problem lies with the situation ($p = .70$) rather than with the employee ($p = .20$). Even if my estimates are wrong, using this as a rule of thumb helps avoid the bias toward attributing problems to employees.

Sometimes ($p = .10$) you will be unable to solve the problem neatly. If unchangeable situational factors are causing a problem, you may have to accept it until change is possible; for instance, if the employee can't access needed tools, you have to accept impaired performance until you can obtain access. If unchangeable employee factors are causing a problem, you'll either have to live with it or replace the person with someone who can perform. For example, if an employee lacks the physical strength to do some aspect of his job, you can accept what he is able to do as good enough, or you can move him to a less demanding job or dismiss him and find someone who is stronger.

Common Causes of Problems

We have been focusing on how to determine that a problem exists, whether it is serious enough to warrant action, and what causes it. Thus far the discussion has been rather abstract, particularly in regard to employee causes. So, let's get more concrete by looking at some examples of common employee causes of problems.

To make things easier, I have divided these common employee causes into four categories: impaired productivity, which is failure to meet output standards; insubordination, which is failure to meet employee-manager behavior standards; annoying behavior, which is failure to meet employee-employee behavior standards; and reactions to diversity, which is failure to meet organizational policy standards. All of these can cause poor performance, either because what the employee does interferes with his or her own performance or because it interferes with the performance of others. In either case, the unit's performance is impaired, reducing its contribution to the organization's overall effort.

Impaired Productivity

Impaired productivity can be caused either by what you do as manager and/or by things that your employees do.

Things You Do

Poor performance by individual employees, or by your unit as a whole, is sometimes attributable to your performance as a manager. In Chapter 1, the Introduction, we said that good managers make six commitments. To refresh your memory, they are:

- *Leadership.* Good managers commit to actively leading their employees.
- *Expectations.* Good managers commit to understanding their own and their employees' work-related expectations and how they affect behavior.
- *Emotions.* Good managers commit to anticipating the emotions that arise from threatened or violated expectations and to dealing with them constructively.
- *Standards.* Good managers commit to translating their expectations about how employees should behave into clear performance standards.
- *Problems.* Good managers commit to carefully evaluating problems that arise when their own and their employees' expectations are not met.
- *Solutions.* Good managers commit to solving problems that arise from unmet expectations promptly, fairly, and effectively.

Failure to make these commitments, or failure to live up to them, will result in a less effective unit and will impair individual employee performance. The fourth commitment, translating your expectations into clear performance standards, has the most direct and concrete impact on performance. If you can't (or won't) think through what you want done and how you want it done, if you can't (or won't) communicate it clearly, and if you can't (or won't) monitor performance to see if your standards are met, you can't (and shouldn't) expect your employees to know what you want and you can't (and shouldn't) expect your standards to be met. The fault is yours, not theirs.

When I was a student, I got a part-time job as a research assistant for a professor who asked me to analyze a large set of data he had gathered as part of a research project. He apparently had more faith than was warranted in the effectiveness of the teaching program; he simply assumed I could do the job because I had recently completed a statistics course. At any rate, he gave me the data and left me on my own. I fumbled around for a long time, finally getting something that looked to me like results, and gave them to him. A single statistics course is almost worse than none; you know just enough to be dangerous. The analysis was all wrong and had to be done over again. The professor was clearly disappointed in me, and I felt awful because I had let him down.

Box 6.3
Wasting Time

A survey by America Online and Salary.com revealed the following to be the most commonly cited ways in which work time is wasted:

✓ Surfing the Internet for personal reasons
✓ Talking with coworkers about topics unrelated to work
✓ Leaving work to run errands
✓ Making personal phone calls
✓ Daydreaming, sleeping, playing computer games, reading, and e-mailing personal messages

The 2,700 respondents to the survey admitted to wasting an average of nearly two hours of work time per day.

Twenty years later, we met again and that failure was the major thing he remembered about our earlier "collaboration." By that time I had learned a lot, among which was the ironclad rule that you do not give employees a task, tell them to do their best, and walk away—unless they're experienced in doing the task they will almost certainly disappoint you.

Things They Do

The other source of impaired productivity is employee behavior that interferes with his or her work or the work of coworkers. Employees that are chronically late to work, take overly long breaks, waste time, stop working before the workday is done, or who frequently leave work early are almost always less productive than they are paid to be. Even if they work hard when they work, their shirking interferes with the productivity of their coworkers, who often need timely information or output that isn't available.

Similarly, missed deadlines, failure to complete work on time, or erratically paced output makes it difficult for coworkers to get their work done on time, decreasing the unit's productivity. Failure to prioritize leads to effort wasted on unimportant tasks while important ones are neglected. Shoddy work requires coworkers to repair it or do it over completely. Excessive e-mail or phone use, especially for private matters, takes time away from work, reduces the person's availability to coworkers, and is a misuse of the organization's communications technology. Although a certain amount of chatting helps maintain social cohesiveness, frequent and excessively long conversations about topics unrelated to work waste time (see Box 6.3). Flirting may seem to its participants like time well spent, but from the unit's viewpoint it isn't.

Malevolent behavior also reduces productivity, thereby undermining the unit's performance. Mistakes and delays occur when workers intentionally convey wrong or misleading information. Employees who engage in malicious gossip, belittling or bullying of coworkers, fostering divisive cliques, seeking attention or special favors from their managers, or otherwise creating tensions that divert energy from work, reduce everybody's productivity.

Employees who don't (or won't) understand the scope of their own jobs also cause performance problems. Some employees narrowly define their jobs, excluding anything not specifically cited in their job description—"That's not my job." In contrast, some tend to encroach on coworkers' jobs, building a little empire of their own. This sometimes is done under the guise of helping the coworker, but once undertaken, the task is never relinquished. Another version is to make up entirely new responsibilities, often giving them priority over genuine job functions, for example, a woman who makes watering the office plants her morning priority even though plant care is contracted with a local florist and her desk is stacked with real work. She wastes time, expects to be thanked for it, and the poor plants nearly drown.

Employees sometimes encroach on their manager's job too, making decisions that are the manager's to make or attempting to manage their coworkers. This almost always causes conflict, either with the manager or with coworkers, and conflict diverts time and effort from productive tasks.

Finally, unit performance deteriorates when employees fail to pull their weight. Almost anything that interferes with an employee's own productivity results in his or her failure to fully contribute to the unit's performance, but sometimes employees make a deliberate effort to avoid doing their share of the work. This reveals itself in passive failures: failure to actively engage in group efforts, failure to contribute ideas or to help develop ideas that others contribute, failure to take responsibility for accomplishing key aspects of the task, failure to carry through on assigned tasks. The employee is willing to share in the credit and other rewards for successful group efforts, but does little to bring that success about; he or she is getting a free ride while the other people do all the work. Free riders don't just fail to contribute, they are a drag on their coworkers, which simply adds to the problem.

Insubordination

Insubordination is a cause of poor individual and unit performance because it makes it difficult for you to coordinate the individual's efforts with the group's and because it introduces conflict. Both of these stem from the fact that insubordination undermines the legitimacy of your authority, thereby interfering with your efforts to promote good performance.

Most organizations have procedures for dealing with outright refusal to perform assigned tasks, often leading to dismissal. These clear challenges to your authority are one thing, particularly with coworkers as witnesses, but when insubordination is more subtle, it often is difficult to make a case for invoking the organization's procedures or arguing for dismissal. For example, you can't fire someone for treating you with undue familiarity, as though you were close friends, however inappropriate it may be. Attempts to undermine your authority when your back is turned are even more difficult to prove—such things as malicious gossip, backbiting, or going over your head to your manager (which may make the person look like a legitimate whistleblower).

Of the various employee-caused problems managers encounter, insubordination may be the hardest to handle, particularly if you and the insubordinate employee are of different ages or different sexes. Older workers often know more than their managers and find it hard to conceal the fact. Men often find it difficult to be supervised by women, and vice versa. One likes to think that gender is becoming less of a workplace issue, but it certainly still exists.

Age differences and experience differences will always exist, and the best you can hope for is to get the experienced worker to help you rather than thwart you. When I was a newly commissioned navy officer, I had to supervise a seasoned chief petty officer who knew far more than I did. I made a point of treating him with respect and asking his advice, without relinquishing decision-making rights. He could have kept me from doing a good job, but he had trained many new officers before me and took pride in doing it well. Like most military people, he showed respect for the officer's rank even when he didn't have a particularly high opinion of the officer. I like to think that he eventually came to respect me, but that was not as important as the fact that he never made his superior knowledge a problem for either of us.

Annoying Behavior

While not illegal or even a violation of the organization's rules, annoying behavior causes performance problems by creating distractions, engendering conflict, or degrading the quality of the workplace. Annoying behavior is annoying because it violates the annoyed employee's expectations about the boundaries of his or her physical or psychological space; annoyance is mild anger. Unfortunately, even trivial violations of their physical/psychological space can sometimes annoy people so much that it has a major impact on their performance.

Distractions

Most distractions involve noise that diverts coworkers' attention from their jobs, usually because it becomes so annoying that everyone focuses on it, and on the anger it engenders, rather than on their work:

- Audible headphones emitting tinny voices or a muffled but persistent drumbeat, perhaps accompanied by the listener humming, singing, or drumming on the desk
- Loud telephone conversations
- Raucous laughter
- Conversations shouted over cubical partitions or down hallways
- Blowing air through the lips or teeth; outright whistling
- Audible talking or singing to oneself
- Undue gusto on the computer keyboard
- Noisy shuffling of paper, clicking of a ballpoint pen, pounding on a stapler, slamming of desk or file cabinet drawers
- Constant wriggling in a creaky desk chair

No doubt you can think of more, but these are the ones that I can list off the top of my head. Considering the aggravation these behaviors cause, it is remarkable that offenders so seldom realize that they are doing anything annoying. Sometimes merely bringing it to their attention is sufficient. But because they usually do it without thinking, more is often required. I know of offices that have installed sound baffles and canned music systems in an effort to cover these noises, sometimes with success. However, some of these sounds seem capable of piercing steel, and mere wallboard (let alone whatever they make cubical walls of) is no match. The only alternative is forbidding whatever causes that particular sound, insisting that noisy work be done in a separate workroom, or replacing squeaky furniture.

Body Functions

I separate these annoyances from distractions because curbing them requires a more subtle approach. This is because, in some cases, the person may be fully aware of the problem but be unable to do anything about it. Loud and persistent burping, flatulence, sniffing, sneezing, coughing, or nose blowing may be annoying but they usually are the result of health issues. Short of medical intervention, there frequently isn't much that can be done aside from isolating the person in some way.

Some bodily annoyances are under the person's control but, like distractions, he or she may not be aware of them, for example, loud yawning, lip smacking, teeth grinding, knuckle cracking, scalp scratching, body odor. Still other annoyances are under the person's control but he or she simply may not realize that the behavior disturbs others, for instance, loud gum chewing, gum popping, nail clipping or nail filing, overdoses of perfume or aftershave (to which some coworkers may be allergic, while others are merely repulsed).

On more than one occasion, I have had to deal with complaints about an employee's persistent and distracting body odor. American culture regards body odor on a par with having a felony conviction. The first time I had to deal with complaints about an odiferous employee, I really did not know how to handle it—I wanted to solve the problem but I didn't want to embarrass him. Finally, taking the bull by the horns, I sat the fellow down and explained the problem. In fact, he was embarrassed, but for an entirely different reason than I expected. It turned out that he had lost his sense of smell. Because he couldn't smell himself or his clothes, he hadn't realized there was a problem. After an awkward moment, he thanked me for telling him and left the room. He solved the problem by changing to a more reliable deodorant and arranging for a friend to check out his clothes before he wore them. In another instance, I had a male employee who strongly believed that real men don't wear deodorants. He agreed to bathe more frequently, and his coworkers stopped complaining.

It is particularly important to deal promptly with customers' and suppliers' complaints about annoying behavior. A clerk who talks to elderly customers in that squeaky little voice most of us reserve for children and small animals may drive your older customers away (and an employee who calls elderly women "Young lady," should be permanently transferred to the mailroom). Someone who treats suppliers and delivery people as though they were dim-witted servants is going to cause trouble. In such cases, the offenders may not even know that they are doing something annoying, and simply pointing it out to them may remedy things. I know a former schoolteacher who spoke to everyone in the simplistic way she had spoken to her first-grade students. When used with adults, this way of speaking comes off as very condescending, and customers found her insufferable. When this unfortunate habit was brought to her attention, she confessed that she was unaware of it. She immediately reverted to compound sentences and words of greater than one syllable, and customer complaints stopped.

Reactions to Diversity

This class of problem-causes reflects the inability of most human beings to feel comfortable around people who are different from them. Social scientists like to point out that humans are tribal animals, comparable in ways to pack animals, such as wolves. We tend to identify with particular groups and to be aggressive toward outsiders.

The group with which we identify usually consists of people who are similar to ourselves. We feel more comfortable with such people because their expectations and ours are similar. As a result, we understand their motives, we can correctly interpret their actions, and we can assume that they are inclined to be friendly toward us. The result is that in our private lives, our friends tend to be similar to us in terms of:

- Income
- Family structure
- Ability levels and intelligence
- Recreational and intellectual interest
- Politics
- Attitudes and morals (particularly about sexual issues and about what constitutes honesty)
- Gender
- Religion (at least broadly)
- Race and, in some cases, ethnicity
- Speech habits
- Attire

The result is that most of us are far more "ghetto-ized" than we realize; we spend most of our private time among people who are pretty much like us because these people tend to be most easily available and because we feel comfortable with them.

In contrast to our private lives, the last fifty years or so has brought broad acceptance of the principle of equal opportunity in education and employment. As a result, workplace homogeneity has increasingly given way to workplace diversity. Today, few people work solely with people like themselves, with the result that few feel completely comfortable, and this sometimes causes difficulties.

In the broadest possible terms, the most common reaction to encounters with people who are different from ourselves is discomfort and an immediate tendency to disapprove of them and their odd ways—they are threatening because we expect them to violate our expectations about how people should behave. Our reaction to the threat is an urge to leave or to make them leave. If neither party can leave, the urge is to change the other person to be as much like ourselves as possible.

Recall what happened when women started moving into management positions. The first reaction on the part of the men who were already there was stunned disbelief, followed by attempts to make the women go away. This was done by ostracizing the women and by demeaning their abilities—women couldn't be trusted with responsibility because their decision making would be impaired when they had their monthly periods or they would be ineffective when their "maternal instincts" prompted them to be too sympathetic to employees. When excluding and demeaning them didn't work, workplace conditions often were made unpleasant. In some cases this took the form of outright sexual harassment. When courts stepped in and held institutions responsible in harassment cases, tactics changed and women were urged to be more like men; we even saw a period when women wore suits that looked like a man's suit but with a skirt instead of pants. All this nonsense lasted until repeated demonstrations of women's managerial abilities revealed the underlying fallacy of thinking that different is necessarily inferior.

Most diversity problems—which typically involve race, religion, gender, or ethnic origin—have been discussed at length in the popular and professional media. We all know about them, but we are always surprised when we come face to face with them. Young employees are far more used to diversity than were their predecessors, and we can hope that diversity problems will become less common in the future. More likely, however, as workplace diversity increases, familiar problems will be replaced by unfamiliar ones or by new versions of the ones we thought we had overcome.

How People Deal with Diversity

Different people deal with workplace diversity in different ways, ranging from embracing it, through tolerating it, to resisting it. Of course, embracing diversity is not going to lead to problems for you as a manager, so it is to be encouraged in whatever ways you can. At the other extreme, resistance is the most obvious source of problems, ranging all the way from passively ignoring people unlike oneself, through doing petty things like insults and slurs, to outright violence. Sexual harassment illustrates this gradation of resistance to women in the workplace. Little things like pinup pictures or dirty jokes make it clear that women are outsiders and are aimed at making them uncomfortable enough to leave. More serious things like demeaning pranks and dirty tricks cause embarrassment or damage to personal property, putting on more pressure to leave. Most extreme is assault, which is all about power and intimidation and is aimed at frightening the woman into leaving. This same gradation of resistance can be observed when the outsider is gay or lesbian, a member of a racial or ethnic minority, or a member of some non-mainstream religion.

Tolerance lies between embracing diversity and resisting it. Tolerance acknowledges differences while attempting to act as though they did not exist. Tolerance too has gradations. At one end is willing tolerance, just short of embracing the differences between oneself and others. At the other end is grudging tolerance, just short of resisting the difference. I once lived in a European country that is celebrated for its tolerance. However, I soon realized that tolerance in this case was a form of indifference—I disapprove of you and your foreign ways, but I'll leave you alone if you leave me alone. It seemed to me that this produced a very strange culture in which those who were born there were a closed group and everybody else was an outsider. Outsiders and their behavior were tolerated but not embraced, which I suppose is what happens in most Western countries; outsiders remain outsiders and insiders congratulate themselves on being so liberal.

In today's workplace, resistance to diversity always causes problems for managers and for the organization, if for no other reason than it absorbs employees' energy and impairs cooperation. Tolerance of diversity is better than resistance, in that the problems it causes usually are inadvertent. Although embracing diversity is to be encouraged, tolerance is sufficient for the organization to function and to keep conflict to an acceptable minimum. Indeed, it may be all you can hope for at the moment; general acceptance of diversity in the workplace is a work in progress.

Getting Your Story Right

The goal of identifying problems, gathering relevant information, and making attributions about the causes is to create an accurate scenario about what happened and why. As we saw in Chapter 3, a scenario is a story you construct to help you know what to expect. In the present case, the scenario serves to integrate what you have learned from your what, where, when, who, and why questions into an account of what you think happened, a story that you expect to be true or nearly true. This scenario can then be used to explain to yourself and to other people what the problem is and what its causes are, which helps you when you decide what to do about it.

We all think in terms of stories, and we tend to readily come to expect plausible stories to be true, perhaps too readily. That isn't to say that we can't distinguish fact from fiction; few of us believe that TV dramas are true. But we often have difficulty in real life because, frankly, it is easier to settle for a plausible scenario than to continue searching for the truth. As a manager who is making decisions that affect the lives of other people, you don't have the luxury of being lazy; you have to work hard to make sure your scenario is as accurate as the available information will allow. This means that you don't settle for the first plausible scenario that comes along. It is difficult to withhold judgment until all the facts are in, especially if you are under pressure to solve the problem quickly. But you must learn to do it.

Withholding judgment not only reduces the chances of jumping to false conclusions, it also signals your employees that you are not rushing to judgment; that you're trying to be as fair and as careful as possible. This assures them you are not just looking for a scapegoat, but are conscientiously doing your job and searching for the truth about the problem and what caused it. If people see that you will settle for any scenario that appears to explain things, even if it's wrong, they will take you for a villain or a fool and distrust you in the future. A manager who is careless about seeking the truth probably is careless about other things as well and, therefore, cannot be relied upon to be fair or just.

Features of a Scenario

The scenario you derive from the information you obtain must have the following features:

- It must revolve around the five W's—what, where, when, who, and why—usually arranged chronologically.
- It must be economical, including only necessary details and excluding irrelevancies.
- It must be coherent, clearly describing the linkage between the problem and its causes, leaving no significant loose ends.
- It must be descriptive and impartial; your emotions or hunches are not relevant.

If you cannot construct a convincing scenario that has these features, you should keep searching for information that will help you either revise the scenario or reject it in favor of some other scenario. A scenario's accuracy is particularly doubtful if it leaves a lot of loose ends—unsatisfactory answers to what, where, when, who, and why—or a cluttered, murky, or unconvincing path from cause to effect.

The Plausibility Trap

Just as it is easy to accept the first plausible scenario that comes along, it is difficult to give up a plausible scenario once it is accepted. Even if it is flawed, and therefore of questionable accuracy, we tend to use it as a point of reference when we gather additional information. Psychologists call this mental set, which means that we get into a set way of thinking about a problem and have difficulty breaking out of it. The power of the initial scenario to trap us lies in its influence on subsequent thinking about the problem and the way we interpret new information. It prompts us to work on revision of the scenario we've got instead of searching for the scenario we should have. This is a perfectly human thing to do, but it has to be resisted or the decisions you base on it will be as flawed as the flawed scenario. Flawed decisions about how to solve a problem will lead to failure to solve it and probably will make things worse or even cause more problems than you started with.

Using the Scenario

The purpose of the scenario is to illuminate the link between the problem you are trying to solve and the causes of that problem so you can break the link. You break the link by changing the conditions that enable the cause to have its effect—to stop whatever is causing the standard to be violated. In some cases these conditions will be the constraints the situation imposes on how employees behave; in other cases they will be constraints the employee(s), and their particular characteristics, impose on their behavior. The scenario should illuminate which of these factors, situation or employee(s), or their interaction, is responsible for the problem. Then you must look at the available remedies, implement one, and change the constraints so that the problem ceases to be a problem.

Consider a hypothetical example: You note that your unit's productivity has decreased for no obvious reason. You question some of your employees and learn that a number of them have fallen behind in their contributions to the unit's effort. A little more inquiry reveals that one employee, George, stands out because everyone else is down-line from him in the production process. Closer questioning reveals that on a number of occasions George has been discovered asleep at his workbench and that the people who need his output to do their jobs are being held up by his failure to produce on time. The result is that the entire unit's performance is negatively affected.

Your "first-impression scenario" is that George is simply goofing off, which decreases his output, which reverberates on down the line, affecting the whole unit's performance. However, George has always been reliable in the past, so you question your first-impression scenario. When you talk to him, you find out that he has a new baby at home and hasn't been getting enough sleep. Moreover, his workspace is small, poorly ventilated, and is isolated from the rest of the unit—he sometimes goes hours on end without seeing anyone else. This combination of factors results in his inability to stay awake, which results in his inability to get his work done.

You really can't change the fact that George has to help his wife take care of the new baby. Of course, you could simply tell him to seek a solution to his sleepless nights and quit sleeping on the job, but what if he tries his best and still ends up asleep? You don't really want to fire an experienced employee if you can avoid it, so you must work with him on a solution. For example, perhaps you could arrange for him to move to a different workspace so he would be around other people. Before you do this, you conduct a "mental simulation," an imaginary scenario that incorporates everything you know but throwing a new workspace into the mix. From this you try to judge if the change in workspace might reasonably be sufficient to stop him from sleeping on the job. If you think it would, you can set about arranging the move and see what happens. If you don't think moving would be enough of a solution—there is still the baby—you have to work with him to come up with something else. (Perhaps he could work different hours, coming in later in the morning when he is relatively rested, or work part-time for a while, allowing you to hire a temporary employee to do his less exacting tasks.) Whatever the solution you select, you are guided by your scenario and your ability to imagine what would happen to production if you were to implement this or that or another solution. Each solution, or various combinations of solutions, allows you to construct a variation on your original scenario and to imagine what would happen if you implemented the solution(s). These imagined outcomes allow you to select the most promising solution(s). In the next chapter we will review the various kinds of solutions available to you.

Summary

To ensure mastery of the material in this chapter, summarize it for yourself by filling in this topic outline.

I. Definition of a Problem   _____

_____

II. Evaluating Performance Problems   _____

_____

    A. First Tool: Ask Questions   _____

    _____

       1. Using the Answers   _____

       _____

    B. Second Tool: Causal Analysis   _____

    _____

1. Attribution Biases _____

_____

2. Self-serving Bias _____

_____

3. Performing a Causal Analysis _____

_____

4. It Depends Where You're Looking _____

_____

III. Common Causes of Problems _____

_____

A. Impaired Productivity _____

_____

1. Things You Do _____

_____

2. Things They Do _____

_____

B. Insubordination _____

_____

C. Annoying Behavior _____

_____

1. Distractions _____

_____

2. Body Functions _____

_____

D. Reactions to Diversity _____

_____

1. How People Deal with Diversity _____

_____

IV. Getting Your Story Right _____

_____

   A. Features of a Scenario _____

   _____

   B. The Plausibility Trap _____

   _____

   C. Using the Scenario _____

   _____

Exercises

1. Return to your three managers and ask them questions about how they determine the causes of problems. Also, ask them about the kinds of problems they encounter in the course of their jobs.

2. Write an essay outlining your views on managing employees, incorporating what you have learned from the text and what you learned in your interviews.

3. Add your essay to your notebook.

Sources and Further Reading

Einhorn, H.J., & Hogarth, R.M. (1986). Judging probable cause. *Psychological Bulletin, 99*, 3–19.

Jungermann, H. (1985). Inferential processes in the construction of scenarios. *Journal of Forecasting, 4*, 321–327.

Kelly, H.H. (1967). Attribution in social psychology. *Nebraska Symposium on Motivation, 15*, 192–238.

Malanchowski, D., & Simonini, J. (2006). *Wasted time at work still costing companies in 2006.* Survey conducted by Salary.com and reported on AOL.com.

Pennington, N., & Hastie, R. (1988). Explanation-based decision making: Effects of memory structure on judgment. *Journal of Experimental Psychology: Learning, Memory and Cognition, 14*, 521–533.

Sutcliffe, K.M., & Weber, K. (2003). The high cost of accurate knowledge. *Harvard Business Review, 81*, 74–82.

Thuring, J., & Jungermann, H. (1986). Constructing and running mental models for inferences about the future. In B. Brehmer, H. Jungermann, P. Lourents, & G. Sevon (Eds.), *New directions in decision research* (pp. 163–174). Amsterdam: Elsevier.

—7—

Solving Problems

*Good managers commit to solving problems that arise from
unmet expectations promptly, fairly, and effectively.*

The causal analysis described in the preceding chapter (Chapter 6) yields
three options for attributing causality in a performance problem. One option
is to attribute the problem to factors in the situation, which means that you
have to change those aspects of the situation that give rise to the problem.
The second option is to attribute it to factors internal to the employee, which
means that you have to change those aspects of the employee that give rise
to the problem, or replace the employee. The third options is to attribute the
problem to a combination of situational factors and factors internal to the
employee, which means you have to change both the situation and the employee using a combination of the strategies you would use for the situation
or the emplcyee separately.

Changing the Situation

There are four aspects of the situation that most commonly give rise to performance problems and that, as a result, require change in order to solve them.
They are the task, the job, the setting, and the incentive structure.

The Task

Poorly explained or poorly designed tasks account for a large proportion of
situation-caused problems. These problems are easily attributed to the employee performing the task, but the flaw lies in how the task was explained,
the process prescribed for doing it, or misunderstandings about what the task

entails. For example, if inexperienced employees are tasked with a large mailing, failure to instruct them about how to arrange envelopes so it is easy to affix addresses and postage, how to efficiently fold mail-outs and insert them into the envelopes, and how to seal the envelopes securely can make a relatively simple task into a dreary undertaking that takes days to complete. The fault lies in the poor instructions rather than the employees themselves.

Similarly, if every sale requires one copy of a handwritten sales slip to be retained by the sales department and other copies to be sent through the internal mail system to the shipping department and inventory control, the process will break down every time sales become brisk, resulting in backlogs and mistakes because the process is too complicated. More to the point, handwriting sales receipts and sending paper copies through the mail are outmoded in this age of electronics; a modern tool is required. None of these problems is attributable to employees, and all of them can be fixed with a little imagination, effort, and, of course, money.

The Job

There are many books on how to design jobs properly, so we need not go into detail here. Suffice it to say that most employees try to meet performance standards in spite of the constraints of a poorly designed job, usually presuming that the design has been thought through by somebody and the constraints are somehow necessary, even when they know things don't work very well. However, working around a bad design just makes the job harder, which requires extra effort to meet performance standards, extra effort that could be otherwise employed to the organization's benefit.

Sometimes the issue isn't poor design as much as no design at all. It is amazing how many people are hired for jobs that are only vaguely defined; they're given some ambiguous goals and left pretty much on their own about how to meet them. If the employee is exceptional, he or she might come up with something as good as a job design expert might do. More often, however, when it's left up to employees, the result isn't what is needed; they undertake tasks that do not serve the organization's needs or they fail to undertake tasks that are needed. Given the vague situation, they are trying to do their best, and the problems that arise from their misdirected efforts are not really their fault.

Even when it is well designed, if coworkers misunderstand what the employee's job actually is, they are bound to be disappointed. When the employee meets requests with, "That's not my job," it just looks like he or she is lazy. I knew a woman who had worked in an organization's travel office and, tiring of the work, transferred into another unit. Unfortunately, people in the new unit assumed that she had been hired for her travel expertise and began to seek help with their travel arrangements. She was in a difficult position. If she helped them, she was adding to her workload. If she refused, it would look like she wasn't doing her job. Her attempts to explain that travel arrangements weren't part of her new job went unheeded until her manager issued an explanatory memo. Even at that, people tried to get help, but she was in a better position to refuse without causing offense.

The Setting

A job setting involves both the physical setting and the social setting in which it must be performed.

Physical Setting

Problems arising from the physical setting result from things like poorly designed workspaces: too many cubicles in a limited space, desks in open areas that invite interruptions and distractions, offices or shops with poor ventilation or poor lighting. Most of these are common problems that workspace designers know how to solve using both their unique experience and the findings of years of human factors research. The problem is that most organizations don't use workspace designers; they either improvise or they use interior decorators. Improvising often produces bad results, and, however valuable they may be in other respects, decorators seldom design workspaces as well as real workspace designers do.

Even though workspace designers are relatively expensive, they are worth it because bad working conditions almost always reduce productivity, which is more expensive in the long run. An office worker who is constantly putting on or taking off her sweater, or who is always fiddling with a heater hidden under her desk, is wasting time and disrupting her work. Similarly, a product engineer who has poor access to crucial reference material ends up wasting time and disrupting her work. Indeed, a waiter who has to walk a long distance to the kitchen, ensuring that the food he serves is cold, is wasting time and producing dissatisfied customers who won't return. The same is true if workers are provided with inadequate tools: unreliable computers, outmoded machinery, inefficient communication systems. Perhaps the cost of inefficiency is small in each individual case, but it adds up in the aggregate.

Some examples of poor workspace design include the following.

A university computer center hired consultants to help users with their technical problems. There was huge demand for the service, and the waiting line got longer as the day progressed. A little research revealed that the average consultation took ten minutes, which was much too long. A workspace designer pointed out that the consultants were sitting at a table with their clients and that when people sit down together at a table, conventional politeness requires them to go through time consuming greeting and parting ceremonies —"Hello, I'm . . . yada, yada," and "How are you doing . . . .yada, yada," and "Well, bye now; come back if . . . yada, yada," and "Have a good day . . . yada, yada," and "You too . . . yada, yada," and "See ya . . . yada, yada," etc. The designer's solution was to put the consultants behind a counter so that clients stood throughout the consultation. Conventional politeness does not demand much ritual for interactions that take place at counters—think about what happens at a checkout counter in a store. Changing the consultants' workspace from a table to a counter, thus eliminating social ceremonies, reduced the average length of consultations from ten minutes to four minutes, and the waiting line got shorter.

A health club was trying to stop the use of its facilities by nonmembers. It installed a gatekeeper who sat at a desk near the entrance and checked membership cards. Things did not work well because the gatekeepers reported they were being threatened into admitting gatecrashers. This resulted in some gatekeepers being fired because they weren't tough enough and others resigning because of stress. A workspace designer suggested doing away with the desk, which placed the seated gatekeeper lower than the standing gatecrasher, making the gatekeeper look up at the gatecrasher who was looking down at the gatekeeper. It turns out that having to look up at someone who is looking down at you can be very intimidating, especially in an already contentious situation. The designer replaced the desk with a tall stool so that, either sitting or standing, the gatekeeper was at eye level with gatecrashers. The claims about threats stopped, firings and resignations stopped, and the gym stopped having trouble with gatecrashers.

Three famous accidents, the sinking of the U.S. submarine *Thresher* in 1963, the Three Mile Island nuclear power plant near meltdown in 1979, and the New York City Blackout in 2003 were exacerbated, if not wholly caused, by poorly designed control displays. In the case of the *Thresher,* investigators concluded that the accident resulted from a flawed piping system, part of which may have been mislabeling of valves so that crewmen thought they were turning them off when in fact they were turning them on, letting water into the boat. By the time the error was detected, the *Thresher* had plunged so deep it literally came apart, killing everyone on board. In the other two cases, the controllers took emergency action by flipping the appropriate switches on their control panels. Signals on the panels confirmed that the switches had been flipped, but, unbeknownst to the controllers, the signals were not connected to the crucial components of the systems, only to the switches on the control panels. Even though the crucial components failed to respond correctly, the signals led the controllers to believe the operation had been carried out. As a result, subsequent containment actions were either ineffective or the opposite of what was required. As usually happens, the controllers were blamed ("human error") rather than the poorly designed control panels—remember the bias toward internal rather than situational attributions for performance problems. It was only later that the truth was discovered. Note too that humans were initially blamed for the world's worst nuclear accident, at Chernobyl, Russia, in 1986. It turned out that, in fact, workers were poorly trained. But, even more important, the flawed design of the RBMK-type reactor made it so unstable that workers had too little time to take corrective action once trouble began.

Social Setting

Problems arising from the social setting are more difficult to identify and harder to solve:

- In some organizations, managers maintain their power by pitting employees against each other, either through outright competition or by less obvious means. This means that teamwork is impossible, and this tempts employees to cut corners to survive. In my experience, competition, especially when the prize is the manager's approval, leads to conflict and high turnover. Even when competition serves a purpose, as when car dealerships give their individual salespeople bonuses based on sales, it makes teamwork almost impossible and it sometimes leads "ethically impaired" individuals to employ questionable tactics in order to win.
- The organization's culture can make it difficult for employees to do their jobs well. Studies show that employees whose values are at variance with the values of the organization and its culture are more likely to dislike their jobs and to quit. Their expectations differ too much from the organization's and too much from what actually happens for them to feel comfortable, so they leave. There really is little you can do about this except to spot it before too much is invested in new employees and gently help them understand what they've gotten themselves into.
- Finally, although this by no means exhausts the list, problems often arise from the failure of some employees to treat other employees with respect. Status differences are common and can be helpful—executives outrank managers, and so on, which helps everyone remember how power is distributed. But, when legitimate differences are accompanied by arrogance and disrespect, it interferes with cooperation and teamwork, reducing

productivity. For example, when an organization's professionals (such as a college's professors, a law firm's partners, or a hospital's physicians) treat support personnel disrespectfully, they often get lower-quality support than they otherwise might. Similarly, when home office employees treat branch office employees as second-class citizens, the resulting friction reduces productivity. I know of several cases in which work was intentionally done poorly in branch offices, causing more work for the home office staff, as revenge for real and perceived ill treatment.

Incentives

It is silly to expect employees to behave in one way if you offer them incentives for behaving in some other way. Many performance problems are incentive problems—employees are doing exactly what they are being rewarded to do, it just isn't what their manager wants them to do. When this happens, the problem lies with the incentive system, not with the employees.

As the word implies, incentives are supposed to motivate employees to act in ways that advance the organization's interests. To be precise, an incentive is an offer of something for behaving in a particular way, and a reward is what is given for having behaved that way. By offering incentives, an organization is attempting to influence its members' expectations and the behavior that follows from those expectations. But, of course, this only works out well if the behavior for which the incentives are offered is the behavior that is actually wanted.

I know a woman who worked her way through college in the customer service center of a large chain of clothing stores. She was one of many workers whose job was to answer written inquiries and complaints from customers. Had the incentive system been rational, these workers would have been rewarded for the quality of the help they offered. Instead, they were rewarded for the number of inquiries and complaints they processed, without regard to outcome. The result was that anything time consuming or complicated was simply logged in as having been resolved and thrown in the wastebasket. Because repeated inquiries and complaints from customers were each counted as completely new, and there was no follow-up, there was no way to detect the poor service quality. Instead of providing incentives for good service, the system offered them an incentive for processing lots of inquiries and having a clean desk at the end of the day. One can imagine customers' frustration, but the poor service was the logical outcome of a foolish incentive system.

As was discussed in Chapter 5, money is only one form of reward, although it is a primary one. Most employees derive far more from their jobs than just their wages. In fact, provided that wages are at least acceptable, workers derive most of their reward from their ability to do a good job and be productive, being able to solve problems and exercise judgment, being part of a successful group, and doing something useful. The motivation derived from these non-monetary rewards, known as the work ethic, is the principal reason employees strive to perform their jobs well. Incentives and rewards that run counter to the work ethic will interfere with motivation to do a good job. Incentives and rewards that are congruent with, and reinforce, the work ethic will increase job satisfaction as well as motivation to do a good job.

Understanding the role of adequate pay and satisfaction of the work ethic in job performance helps us understand why threats and penalties don't work—at least in the long run. Indeed, threats are negative incentives and penalties are negative rewards. But they don't work the same way as positive incentives and positive rewards, because they interfere with the work ethic—you cannot feel good about doing a good job if it is done under threat, if it is done to avoid penalties rather than for the satisfaction of doing it well. True enough, like incentives and rewards, threats are messages, but they're not the right message—they say to the employee that his or her job isn't a job he or she actually wants. Employees who have no other options will knuckle under to threat and will endure penalties, but those who may have precisely the skills and enterprise you want in your unit will look for more attractive options and soon will move on.

Changing the Employee

If the problem you are trying to solve is caused by the employees, you must focus your energies on changing them in a way that solves the problem. You have a number of tools for doing this. Successive tools represent an escalating response to the problem, and you want to match the magnitude of the response to the magnitude of the problem. Normally, you don't simply fire someone for incessantly popping their chewing gum, no matter how much it irks the person's coworkers. On the other hand, theft or violence requires an immediate and drastic response.

Suiting your response to the problem's magnitude can be tricky. Under-response won't solve the problem and makes you look ineffective. Over-response risks creating a martyr in the eyes of coworkers—they may not like the person's behavior but they seldom want to see him or her treated harshly.

Your Arsenal

In order of severity, your arsenal of responses to problem behavior consists of:

- *Talking,* which is always the first phase in any intervention, preceding the use of any of the other tools in your arsenal. It involves holding a private meeting in which you discuss the problem with the employee and try to determine if it results from unintentional behavior, intentional behavior, or lack of appropriate skills. When the behavior is under the employee's control, this meeting moves into the solution phase that will be described below.

- *Remediation,* which involves training classes or on-the-job training to help the employee acquire the skills required to solve the problem.
- *Reassignment,* which involves giving the employee new responsibilities or a new job that will make the problem behavior either irrelevant or impossible.
- *Discipline,* which involves imposition of penalties for failure to change problem behavior. Some options are reprimands, fines, suspension (with or without pay) for some period, a cut in pay, or demotion, depending on what is provided in your organization's rules and policies.
- *Dismissal,* which involves termination of employment.

Talking

Because talking with the employee always is the first step, it is crucial that it be done correctly. If the employee is unaware of causing a problem, talking frequently is sufficient; you merely need to point out what is wrong and discuss alternatives that will make things better—and it's best if employees come up with the alternatives themselves. If, on the other hand, the behavior is intentional, motives become important. For example, I once supervised a man who was rude and abusive to trainees. He truly believed that what he was doing was right; that he was toughening them up so they could deal with jobs that probably would be quite difficult. In fact, contrary to his expectations, he was discouraging them so much they were dropping out or striving to keep such a low profile that they weren't getting the training they needed. The trainer was sincerely well intentioned, but the behavior that followed from those intentions was destructive. We talked about it, repeatedly, until he realized what he was doing was counterproductive. He still worried that he wouldn't turn out employees tough enough to survive in the real world, but he grudgingly cut back on the abuse. I always thought he could have cut back a lot more, but he was in other ways an excellent trainer and the dropout rate went down, so I settled for what I could get.

Talking with employees about performance problems is difficult. Most managers go to extremes; they are either too tough, making accusations and threats, or too soft, making apologies and offering compromises. The secret is to regard the talk as part of your job, nothing personal, and to hit a happy medium between tough and soft. Box 7.1 describes how to conduct the talk (pages 150–151).

Remediation

Not infrequently, employees' problems turn out to result from simple inability to do what is asked of them. (An unanticipated danger of concocting an exaggerated résumé is getting hired for a job you can't do.) Sometimes employees are so self-confident that they don't even realize how badly they fall short of your standards. We all have known cases in which someone was fired or moved to another job, leaving ruin in their wake while never seeming to understand the damage they had done.

I once knew a woman who was hired to manage data for a large research project. Her résumé looked good and her references seemed solid. However, it soon became evident that both her résumé and her references were misleading; she had no idea how to manage data. Attempts at remediation, to help her learn on the job, were met with resistance and hostility. Finally, everything having been exhausted, she was dismissed. She still refused to accept that she was at fault, so she sued for wrongful termination. (Because her manager had documented everything, the former employee lost the lawsuit.)

Remediation can be done in a number of ways. Some organizations enroll employees in courses offered by local colleges, commercial training schools, or on-line providers. Large organizations often offer their own in-house training programs. In most cases, managers arrange through Human Resources for their employees to take such courses.

On a less formal level, managers often solve the remediation problem themselves by assigning the employee to a mentor who helps him or her learn on the job. This requires an experienced employee who is willing to be a mentor, either as part of his or her job or for extra compensation. It also takes a willingness on the part of the problem employee to be mentored. It often takes a good deal of diplomacy to get an employee to take genuine advantage of remediation. If the employee sees the remedial training as a punishment, he or she is likely to resent having to do it and is unlikely to profit from it (like most people feel about going to traffic school after a fender-bender). Anybody can sit through a course without learning or can thwart attempts at on-the-job training. You have to make it clear that failure to improve by a specific deadline will have negative consequences. And, of course, failure to meet the deadline must actually trigger those consequences.

Reassignment

Sometimes talking and remediation are insufficient. It may well be that with all the goodwill in the world the employee is powerless to change his or her behavior. When this is the case, you have an option of changing the employee's

Box 7.1

How to Talk with an Employee about a Performance Problem

Preparing for the Talk

✓ Keep in mind that your goal is to change the employee's behavior or to instruct the employee about how to behave, not to change his or her beliefs, values, or personality.

✓ Know the facts (your scenario):
   • What is the nature of the performance problem and what are the implications?
   • What is the nature of the behavior that causes the performance problem?
   • Approximately how often does this behavior happen?
   • When did it happen last and what were the consequences?
   • What is available to you to deal with failure to change the behavior that causes the problem (reprimand, fine, suspension, pay cut, demotion, and dismissal)?

Conducting the Talk

✓ Conduct the meeting in private and on your turf (for example, your office), which gives you something of a moral advantage. Never conduct the talk, or anything related to it, in front of coworkers—humiliation is not an acceptable tactic.

   ✓ It often is wise to have someone else, such as a secretary, within earshot so that charges of inappropriate behavior on your part cannot be made later. This is awkward because it compromises the confidentiality of the talk, but in this litigious world, it is a good idea. I have always found it enough to leave the door open slightly so the secretary can hear the tone of your voices and significant silences, rather than hearing what is actually said. I always tell the employee with whom I am talking that I am leaving the door ajar. Never secretly record the talk, even if you think you might need to protect yourself—if things are that serious, openly record the meeting or have a neutral third party physically present, with the employee's permission.

✓ Get to the point immediately. Attempts to lighten the mood by making jokes or small talk make you look hesitant and trivialize the problem so subsequent steps are likely to seem disproportionately drastic.

✓ Take your time and give the talk your full attention. Do not take telephone calls or permit other distractions.

✓ Be professional; don't blame your own manager or other employees for making you have the talk. However uncomfortable you may be, take responsibility for doing what is, after all, your job. Attempting to pass the buck just makes you look pathetic.

✓ Based on your scenario, describe the behavior in question, the problem it causes, and the implications of the problem for the unit and the organization. Stick to the issue; don't muddle things by bringing up other behaviors or other problems.

✓ Listen closely to the employee's rebuttal and give it genuine, objective consideration.

✓ In light of your understanding of the problem and the employee's rebuttal, ask for clearly defined behavioral changes.

✓ Set specific deadlines for accomplishment of the behavioral changes.

✓ State the precise consequences of failure to meet the deadlines.

✓ Describe the consequences in straightforward, non-vindictive terms; angry threats are counterproductive. The point is not to coerce, it is to help the employee understand that behavior has consequences and that he or she can control those consequences by what he or she does.

✓ By asking specific questions, make sure the employee understands what is being asked of him or her, the deadlines, and the consequence of noncompliance.

✓ Expect the employee to be unhappy and allow him or her to express those feelings, so long as he or she maintains self-control. Shouting and threats are unacceptable; try to calm the employee, but if you fail, terminate the talk immediately—leave the room and call security if necessary.

✓ Have tissues available in case of tears.

✓ Try to conclude on a friendly note, but don't back down or reduce the impact of what has gone before by being overly conciliatory.

Follow-up

✓ Finally, and this is of crucial importance, make a point of checking to see that the problem behavior has changed by the deadline. If not, make sure the promised consequences occur, or you will lose credibility.

✓ Do not give second chances unless there is a genuine and compelling reason for doing so or you will lose credibility. Loss of credibility with the employee means you lose all leverage in subsequent attempts to solve the problem. Even worse, when the employee's coworkers learn about your failure, you lose both their respect and any hope you have of dealing with problems involving them.

responsibilities so that the problem behavior ceases to be a problem, usually because it becomes irrelevant. For example, a receptionist who does not speak clearly on the telephone can be assigned different duties and someone else can take over the phones. Perhaps diction lessons would help, but the expense probably is difficult to justify if there is another job the employee can do well and he or she is willing to switch to it. You have to be careful not to imply that the change is punishment or a demotion, but you have to be clear that things can't go on as they are.

Of course, changing employees' responsibilities is essentially the same thing as moving them to another job; they just stay in your unit, perhaps at the same workstation. Sometimes, however, it is best to help them move to a job somewhere else in the organization, especially if their coworkers harbor ill will as a result of the problems they caused. Usually these lateral transfers require the cooperation of the human resources office, but I have often seen deals made between managers that ended in trades that helped both of them solve their employee problems, with Human Resources being brought in to clinch the deal.

It always is tempting to urge problem employees to apply for better jobs elsewhere and to write glowing letters of support, just to get rid of them. This is common in large bureaucratic organizations, which accounts for why they often don't function very efficiently. This practice has made recommendations nearly useless and hiring a lot more difficult. The best rule is to write the recommendation for a departing employee that you would like to receive if you were considering that person for a job. Of course, in a litigious environment, this may be a hard rule to follow.

Discipline

Both remediation and reassignment can be consequences of being unable to meet a deadline for changing problem behavior, but they should not imply that the employee is somehow in the wrong—they just need help. On the other hand, when the behavior is under the employee's control and he or she fails to change it, the consequences are, quite simply, punishment for having failed. However, punishment is not revenge. (Punishment offers the opportunity to try again, to avoid future punishment, but revenge is an end in itself.) Revenge has no place in your arsenal.

The kinds of discipline that are available to managers vary from one organization to another and within levels of any single organization. Usually, the CEO doesn't discipline vice presidents by docking their pay, but department heads sometimes dock their employees' pay. Many organizations don't allow fines, but the baseball industry does, for example. Suspensions, with or without pay, are not uncommon, although they often occur during investigations of serious problems, such as suspected embezzlement. You seldom can demand the employee do more work or put in longer hours for the same pay—the equivalent of writing an extra term paper or staying after school. Depending on their classification, you can ask some employees to work extra to clean up any messes their problem behavior has caused. Sometimes you can demand apologies to employees who have been harmed by the problem behavior, but this smacks of humiliation and should be used carefully.

The fact is, legal actions have narrowed the list of disciplinary measures available to managers. The result is that most measures are part of a chain that can lead to dismissal rather than penalties in and of themselves. The first step in the disciplinary chain consists of a verbal warning to change the behavior, which takes place during the talk. If this fails, the second step consists of a written warning, which is added to the employee's file and which contributes to the "paper trail" of documentation that can eventually lead to dismissal. Short of dismissal, the third step sometimes consists of suspension without pay, again duly documented in the employee's file. Continual failure leads to the final step, dismissal.

Dismissal

Most managers do not have the power to dismiss employees on their own. However, by preparing the paper trail that documents the initial problem and the steps that were taken to remedy it, the manager is in a position to recommend that the employee be dismissed. Usually, the manager has been in contact with Human Resources throughout the effort to solve the problem and has received advice about what documentation to amass. Thus, when the time comes, everything is in place and the dismissal can take place reasonably smoothly and without fear of legal repercussions.

Not having the responsibility for actually dismissing the employee is not the same as not being responsible for telling him or her that it is happening. Of all the duties a manager has, delivering this news has to be one of the toughest.

On the other hand, if you have done your job properly, following the procedures described above and keeping Human Resources informed, being dismissed is not likely to come as a surprise to the employee; he or she should have seen it coming. (None of which makes it easier to tell the employee that the decision has been made.)

Some organizations simply send a termination letter through the mail, usually as a registered letter so they know it was received. This is rather cowardly, it seems to me. The employee deserves the courtesy of a little personal attention right at the end, and you have been working with him or her on the problem up to this point, so it is your job.

There always has to be a formal termination letter from someone in the organization, usually the vice president for human resources or maybe the CEO. You should have a copy of it with you when you meet with the employee to notify them that they have been dismissed. The professionalism and directness required for your first talk about the problem also are required for this final talk. You also need the same clarity about the finality of what is happening; no second chances. Be as supportive as you can; being fired is an emotional event. But don't be overly conciliatory and don't countenance shouting or an angry outburst. You must be in control of the situation because the employee may not be able to control his or her emotions. You need firm understanding and a box of tissues.

Begin by briefly recounting what has led to this point. Give terminated employees the letter as you tell them that they are dismissed. Then, give them instructions about what to do next. Perhaps they have to check with payroll to pick up their last check. They may have to complete paperwork in the human resources office. They have to remove their personal possessions from their workspace and, perhaps, from a locker. Some organizations insist that they vacate the building by a certain time, even assigning security employees to accompany them from the time they leave your meeting until they leave the premises. Indeed, some even forbid them from returning to the premises in order to guard against sabotage or other forms of revenge.

My private opinion is that organizations often get carried away with prevention of lawsuits and revenge. I once had to dismiss an employee who had been padding his expense account. A whistleblower brought it to my attention, and there was a clear paper trail documenting the seriousness of what had been done. I confess to mixed emotions. What the man had done was wrong, but I also found out that his wife had recently left him, taking the house and money, and he had been drinking heavily. But my organization's lawyer was new on the job and was trying to prove she was tough. She ordered me to go to his office, deliver his termination letter, verbally inform him he was fired, and tell him to immediately leave the building, not to return under threat of being arrested for trespassing; his personal possessions were to be sent to him later. Moreover, I was not to engage in any conversation with him. My job was simply to make sure he was out as soon as possible.

I was appalled. I had worked with the man for two years. I felt sorry about his personal problems. On the other hand, I was very disappointed in him; there was no excuse for what he had done—the amount of money was, in fact, rather small. I had to do what the lawyer ordered me to do, but I vowed I would never participate in such a coldhearted procedure again.

Of course, even when you want to dismiss someone, it doesn't always work out. I once took over for a manager who was on leave for a year. It soon became clear that one of the employees was a liability. She was aggressive, noisy, disruptive, and tended to take over other employees' jobs, which she was convinced they were too dumb to do properly. People closed their office doors to avoid her, but she was so overwhelming, so intimidating that nobody actually did anything about her—including her regular manager. I talked to her repeatedly, but couldn't get through; she simply told me I was wrong. Because things couldn't continue as they were, I began to put together documentation for her dismissal. This took a while because nothing before had been documented. On the very day I was to take the documentation to my boss to get permission to dismiss her, she was voted Employee of the Month by her coworkers, in the most rigged election I've ever seen. What could I do? The award looked legitimate, and it eloquently refuted my documentation. Stymied, I quietly dropped my plan and the unit endured her for six more months before she found a job elsewhere.

Dismissal is a serious matter and should be your solution of last resort. Aside from the toll it takes on you to do it, dismissal has a negative impact on a lot of other people—the person, of course, as well as his or her family, friends, and coworkers. Being dismissed usually has a financial impact, and it often decreases the person's worth in his or her own eyes as well as in the eyes of family and friends. Even if the person finds a new job quickly, it can take a long time to recover financially from even a small gap in income flow. Emotional reactions to dismissal can break up marriages, cause health problems, and destroy friendships—particularly friendships with former coworkers.

Dismissing an employee also takes a toll on your unit. On the one hand, dismissing someone who is a source of problems may improve things; on the other hand, the other employees have to take up the slack until a replacement is found and can get up to speed. Moreover, coworkers often feel threatened and insecure when someone is fired; it reminds them that they too are vulnerable. This is particularly true if they have not been allowed to see all the steps that were taken to solve the problem before you had to resort to dismissal; which is to say, when they fear that you have been arbitrary or unfair in deciding to dismiss the person.

The Importance of Fairness

Organizations run on rules, and the essence of fairness is that everybody is subject to the same set of rules unless there are explicit and justifiable exceptions. Indeed, corruption can be defined as the illegitimate use of different rules for different people. Employees perceive managers' actions to be unfair when they think the rules have been ignored or have been applied corruptly.

Fairness is central to everything you do as a manager. If employees decide you do not deal fairly with them, they will stop trusting you. To lose trust is to lose everything because it reduces you to threats and punishment. (Even threats won't work if employees don't trust that you will carry through.)

Scientists have extensively examined fairness in the workplace, and their conclusions are useful for managers. One thing they have discovered is that perceived unfairness is a major cause of dissatisfaction with the job and the organization—which results in increased turnover. In addition, perceived unfairness makes supervision more difficult because employees are indignant about past decisions and distrust future decisions. Furthermore, it is divisive to the unit, because it frequently involves some employees being treated better than others, resulting in jealousy and resentment. This sours the unit's climate, making teamwork more difficult. In short, perceived unfairness corrodes everything.

The corrosive climate induced by perceived unfairness is easy to detect. Altruistic behavior decreases in a climate of distrust. People become less courteous, less helpful, less conscientious, less willing to follow the rules, more selfish and less willing to go the extra mile, less tolerant and more irritable, quicker to complain and to find fault, and they become less willing to participate in the day-to-day activities that make the unit function pleasantly and effectively.

The first place that fairness is important is in the process used to decide whether a problem exists or not and, if so, how serious it is (Chapter 6). Employees have to believe that you are not out to find problems that do not exist, that you are not exaggerating the seriousness of small problems, and that you aren't looking for scapegoats. Solving problems involves change, and change is difficult on people; it takes energy away from their jobs, and they are unlikely to cooperate if they don't think it's necessary.

The second place that fairness is important is in the decision about a problem's causes: situation or employee. Employees have to believe that you are not biased toward blaming them for problems, that you have an open mind about situational causes. Their natural bias is to attribute their own performance problems to situational causes, so they are inclined to see you as being unfair if you attribute their problems to them rather than the situation. This means that you have to be scrupulously fair, and clearly be seen to be fair, when making causal attributions.

The third place that fairness is important is in the decision about how you solve the problem. Even if your solution involves changing the situation, the burden of change must be fair to everyone involved or they will feel you have acted unjustly. For example, if you decide that an employee is under-producing because he has an outmoded computer, purchasing him a new one may cause others to see him as being favored and themselves being deprived. The solution may cause a bigger problem than the one it is intended to solve.

Scientists divide perceived unfairness (which they call "organizational justice") into two categories, distributional fairness and procedural fairness.

Distributional Fairness

People appear to evaluate the fairness of how rewards (pay, bonuses, privileges, etc.) or penalties (pay cuts, withdrawal of privileges, etc.) are distributed in terms of equity, equality, or need. Equity means that they think it is fair for rewards to be contingent on level of contribution and penalties to be contingent on level of culpability, so someone who works hard deserves more than someone who doesn't and someone who causes more trouble than others deserves greater punishment.

Equality means that everyone shares equally in the rewards for successes and suffers equally for failures. Equal rewards often are given to the members of successful teams because it often is difficult to calculate the relative contributions of the various members. (But, when such calculations are possible, a policy of equal rewards is likely to distress those who make the greatest contributions—even those who contribute less are often distressed when they receive the same reward as the big contributors.) With the possible exception of the team leader, who often assumes more blame, it is common for the members of unsuccessful teams to take equal blame as well as an equal share of the penalties, even if they didn't all contribute equally to the failure.

In contrast to equity and equality, people often are willing to tolerate, even encourage, "unfair" distribution of rewards if some members of the group are legitimately in greater need than they are. However, there are limits to their charity; they usually would prefer equitable or equal distribution of rewards, after which they can decide how much of their share to contribute to the needy. (Coerced charity is seldom seen as fair.) When things go wrong, they often think the strong should take a greater "hit" than the weak. For example, when pay cuts are unavoidable, they may think that the more highly paid people ought to be cut more than those who are paid the least.

Procedural Fairness

People usually are even more concerned with fairness in relation to how rewards are distributed than they are in relation to the final distribution. That is, even if they don't like the distribution, if they believe that the process that led to it was fair, they are less distressed than if they think the process was flawed (see Box 7.2). People appear to evaluate procedural fairness in terms of process fairness and moral fairness.

Process fairness means that the process that led to the distribution of rewards or punishments was seen to follow clear, preestablished rules. If the rules weren't followed, the process will be judged to be unfair and the resulting distribution of rewards or punishments will be judged to be unfair. Generally, the remedy for process unfairness is compensation for those who were wronged by it and punishment for whoever did it.

Moral fairness means that, even if the rules are followed, if the final distribution of rewards or punishments violates employees' beliefs and values, the distribution will be judged to be unfair. This usually means that the rules, or how they are applied, must be changed. For example, if employees value the idea that everyone should be paid the same for doing comparable jobs, then a distribution in which women receive less than men will be judged to be morally unfair. Even if the organization's rules clearly state that women will be paid less (implausible as that might be), these employees will be dissatisfied and argue for a change in the rules.

Moral fairness also includes how the rules are applied. If someone is treated rudely, gratuitously demeaned, or intentionally embarrassed during the decision about rewards or punishments, the whole thing will be seen as morally unfair. Generally, the remedy for moral unfairness requires, in addition to compensation for the wronged person(s), that the transgressor be punished and be required to make an apology.

Implications for Solving Performance Problems

Research on fairness tends to focus on the distribution of rewards, like pay raises, bonuses, pay cuts, and the like. However, the results contribute, if somewhat obliquely, to our earlier discussion about deciding on and implementing solutions to performance problems.

Let us assume you have taken over a unit of an organization that has very clear rules about annual performance evaluations and the resulting annual raises, but does not provide rules for dealing with performance problems throughout the rest of the year. It is assumed by your bosses that you will find a way, because that's your job.

So, taking the bull by the horns, you meet with your employees and initiate a discussion about how to deal with problems before they get so large that they impact the annual evaluations and pay raises. You tell them that you'd like to have a clear list of rules about how you, and they, should go about solving these problems, and ask if they have any suggestions. Listen closely to the suggestions and then go away and incorporate them into a draft policy state-

Box 7.2
Guidelines for Fairness

There are five guidelines for ensuring that you are fair to your employees:

1. **Treat employees with dignity and respect.** This isn't just the right thing to do, it also encourages them to give you the benefit of the doubt if you inadvertently make errors that they otherwise would regard as unfair.
2. **Make every effort to change rules that result in unfairness.**
3. **Follow the rules, if rules exist.** If the organization doesn't provide rules for decision making about rewards and punishments, establish them for your unit and make them available to your employees before the decisions are made. Do this early enough that the flaws can be discovered and fixed. Then, follow your rules and make the entire procedure as transparent as possible. Your rules should:
   - ✓ Provide enough detail that you can use the same rules consistently in the future;
   - ✓ Provide employees with a way of providing input prior to decisions being made;
   - ✓ Provide a way of verifying all the information to be used in decisions;
   - ✓ Provide a way for countering your own biases toward attributing problems to people and toward downplaying your own role in causing problems;
   - ✓ Provide a mechanism for giving explanations to employees about decisions pertaining to them;
   - ✓ Provide a mechanism for employees to appeal provisional decisions so corrections can be made before final decisions are made;
   - ✓ Provide objective ethical oversight by a disinterested party so you don't get caught up in moral unfairness.
4. **Stick to your decision once the appeals have been heard and a final decision has been made.** Subsequent tinkering on a case-by-case basis simply causes confusion and makes you look weak. On the other hand, if a real injustice comes to light after everything is settled, you must deal with it. If it requires monetary compensation, make cuts elsewhere in your budget to honor your obligation. If it requires an apology, make it with as much grace and goodwill as you can; it is okay to admit you've made a mistake if it wasn't motivated by malice. If it was malicious, admit your mistake and apologize anyway; you deserve to be embarrassed.
5. **Learn from your errors.** No matter what you do, you will make errors —hopefully not so large they can't be fixed. Learn from them and don't let them happen again. Albert Einstein is supposed to have observed that insanity is doing the same thing repeatedly and expecting a different result. Change your rules if they lead to unfair decisions; lobby to change the organization's rules if they make you make unfair decisions.

ment for your unit. Invite comment, incorporate the comments into the draft, and produce a final document that can be distributed throughout the unit.

Keep the rules simple. For example:

- When it comes to my attention that the unit's performance is threatened, I will begin an inquiry into the causes.
- The inquiry will begin with a search for relevant information from records and discussions with relevant members of the unit.
- Depending on the seriousness of the problem and what is learned in the inquiry, I will either proceed on my own or form a committee of representatives of the unit to help me find the cause(s) of the problem and to help me craft an appropriate solution.
- If it is decided that the problem is attributable to factors in the work situation, steps will be taken to change those factors while avoiding the creation of yet other problems.
- If it is decided that the problem is attributable to factors involving one or more employees, steps will be taken to change those factors in a respectful yet effective manner.

You may want to add detail specific to your unit, but avoid getting too complicated. The more detail you include, the more constrained you will be when it comes time to apply the rules. Remember, violations of these rules will be regarded as unfair; unnecessary detail just provides more opportunities for critics to say you unfairly violated your own rules.

Okay, you have a set of rules for dealing with performance problems. A short time later you have an employee whose performance has slipped so much it is impairing the unit's performance. You must solve the problem in a way that is fair in both fact and appearance—the employee must think you have been fair and your other employees must think so too.

You begin by getting your facts straight and making sure the employee is the cause of the problem rather than the situation (Chapter 6). Then you talk with him and tell him about your concerns and ask for suggestions about how he can improve his performance. You agree on specific improvements, the deadlines by which they are to be achieved, and the penalties for failure to achieve them on time. If, in fact, he doesn't meet the deadlines and has no convincing excuse, you must impose the penalties.

The purpose of this first round of deadlines and penalties was to encourage the desired improvement, so the penalties should be the weakest ones in your arsenal. If, in fact, he fell short and incurred the penalties, it is time to talk about what will happen if he continues to fail—new deadlines and new penalties. You should allow only one or two rounds of this, increasing the severity of the penalties each time, before you impose the most severe penalties.

The Ultimate Test of Fairness: Downsizing

Sometimes your employees' and the unit's performance are perfectly adequate but the organization's strategy or its economic circumstances change. Minor shifts in strategy usually are taken in stride, and people make the necessary changes without much more than a little grumbling. Performance of the new or modified responsibilities may take a while to get up to speed, but, with your help and encouragement, adjustment to minor change usually goes reasonably smoothly.

Big change is something else, in large part because it frequently involves "downsizing" in order to decrease labor costs. This means that some of your employees are going to be faced with a choice between transferring to a new job in a different unit or becoming unemployed. Others won't even have that choice; their jobs simply will cease to exist. Of course, it is your responsibility to fight for the least possible negative impact on your employees and your unit, but even a good fight is unlikely to fully protect them.

Unit managers seldom make the decision to downsize on their own, but sometimes are forced to decide who will go and who will stay. Moreover, they usually have to deliver the bad news to those who must go, and afterward have to deal with the fears and emotions of those who stay.

Transfers and Layoffs

Shifts in organizational strategy often involve creation of new units and changing the sizes of old ones. When orders come to downsize your unit, it may be possible to work with Human Resources to place some of your people in one of the new or expanding units. Where possible, most organizations prefer to salvage the experience and talents of their existing personnel, so the opportunity to transfer some of your people should not be overlooked—in this you should be an advocate for your employees, looking out for their interests and making sure that they have access to other jobs if they want them.

Sometimes, however, the organization undergoes such a severe shift in strategy that many skills become obsolete. Or, the strategy may be merely to what it has been doing but with fewer people in order to cut costs. In these cases, people must be laid off, and it probably will be you who gives them the bad news.

Of course, the easiest way to lay someone off is simply to send him or her a letter containing the dreaded "pink slip." Easiest isn't best, because it is bound to lead to complications—bad publicity for the organization and wrongful termination suits, among other things. Moreover, when the people who didn't get laid off hear about the brusque, rude, heartless, and so forth, way in which layoffs were done, they are going to be angry. A lot of that anger is going to be directed at you if you sent the letter.

Researchers have examined at length the conditions that give rise to hostile reactions to layoffs, both on the part of the "victims" and the "survivors." Of course, those two terms are pretty loaded, but most of us tend to sympathize with employees who lose their jobs for no reason of their own, and the employees who remain after a round of layoffs often view themselves very much as survivors.

Of course, nobody likes being laid off and nobody likes having a friend laid off. There is bound to be a lot of emotion—primarily anger at what can appear as arbitrariness and a heartless betrayal by an organization to which they committed themselves. At the least, this anger impacts morale and makes people consider leaving. At the extreme, this anger can result in violence, sabotage, public denunciation of the organization and its policies, and other forms of retaliation. In either case, anger often results in psychological and behavioral problems as people try to adjust to the change. The key to keeping anger from getting out of hand lies in handling the layoffs, and the aftermath, with humanity and good sense. The Manager's Golden Rule applies: Treat your employees, both victims and survivors, as you would want to be treated. The keys are communication, transparency, and fairness:

- Advanced notice that layoffs are coming
- Careful explanation of why the organization must downsize
- Criteria for deciding who will be laid off
- Alternatives available to those who are to be laid off; transfer opportunities and outplacement assistance
- Information about severance packages and options for health care, retirement funds, and so on
- Timelines for when decisions will be made and when notification will occur, as well as how notification will occur

Unionized workplaces usually handle advanced notice pretty well because the organization has to negotiate with the union prior to doing anything. Once the union is informed, the workers are quick to know. However, it is in the organization's interests to explain its position itself, rather than leaving things up to the union, although it is crucial for the union to be involved as much as possible. The union's credibility ensures that the layoffs are not seen as the result of an arbitrary management decision.

In the absence of a union, management often issues written statements about the problems the organization faces and how layoffs are necessitated by those problems. Written statements are notoriously poor ways of conveying threatening news—people have a way of never reading beyond the bad news, so they miss the reasons for it. It is far better if the unit managers meet with their employees and go over the same information verbally, allowing time for discussion. The opportunity to discuss the threat, to submit questions to you and through you to higher management, as well as to generally vent emotions, helps defuse the anger that will build as the layoff process unfolds.

In all of this, your job is to be as humane and as supportive of your employees as possible, without joining the inevitable grumbling and complaining. You don't have to pretend to like what is happening, but you shouldn't try to appease your employees' anger and fear by joining them in damning the organization. It probably is true that you don't agree with the decision to downsize—it is bound to make your life harder—but it is your job to carry it out. You must walk a fine line between being supportive and fostering conspiracy, between being sympathetic and fanning the flames of resentment.

When the final decisions have been made about who is to be laid off, you should meet with each individual and tell him or her face to face before he or she receives a formal notice. Treat the layoff interview just as you do all the others—do it in a private place, be professional, don't offer excuses but explain the criteria used to decide to lay some employees off but not others, let the employee express emotions (remember to have tissues handy) but don't let his or her emotions sway you. Be kind, but be firm—don't hold out false hope. Direct him or her to whatever outplacement services the organization provides. Finish the interview by telling him or her precisely what to do next—pick up the last check at payroll, go to the benefits office to arrange for health care, clean out his or her workspace and take personal items away, and all the rest. If the organization dictates that laid-off employees are not to be left alone until they depart or are not to be allowed back on the property after they leave, explain why this measure has been adopted (it usually is to avoid sabotage or violence); "Although we both know that the measure isn't necessary in your case." This business of escorting laid-off employees from the premises and barring their return is one of the most degrading things organizations do. It can undo all the good work invested to reduce the trauma of being laid off. Moreover, it probably is far less necessary than lawyers seem to think—resist doing it if you can, be gentle if you can't.

The aftershock of layoffs can be almost as bad as the thing itself. Survivors often are badly shaken by what they regard as a near miss. On the one hand they feel relief because they still have a job. On the other hand they feel guilt about having survived while friends and coworkers got laid off. These conflicting emotions can be very strong and can severely interfere with job performance—people often have to seek counseling. The responsibility for dealing with this fallout will fall mainly on you.

Even if the organization provides counseling for survivors, the real key is prevention. And prevention involves doing much the same things for survivors as you did for the people who were laid off: Advanced information, thorough explanation, description of the criteria for decisions about who goes and who stays, and all the rest. It also helps if survivors know that nobody in the organization enjoyed the exercise; you probably won't have any trouble convincing them that you didn't want to lay anyone off, but, again, you mustn't overdo it.

So, it all boils down to behaving well—helping employees through a difficult time and then getting the unit back into action and bringing productivity up to the desired level as soon as possible. If you, (and the organization) behave well, survivors will retain their trust in you and, if you'll recall, trust is key to being an effective manager. If you behave badly and lose their trust, it will complicate your job no end. Moreover, it will take a long time to get that trust back, and none of that time will be much fun.

Summary

To ensure mastery of the material in this chapter, summarize it for yourself by filling in this topic outline.

I. Options for Causal Attribution and Action _____

_____

II. Changing the Situation _____

_____

    A. The Task _____

    _____

    B. The Job _____

    _____

    C. The Setting _____

    _____

        1. Physical Setting _____

        _____

        2. Social Setting _____

        _____

D. Incentives _____

_____

III. Changing the Employee _____

_____

A. Your Arsenal _____

_____

1. Talking _____

_____

2. Remediation _____

_____

3. Reassignment _____

_____

4. Discipline _____

_____

5. Dismissal _____

_____

IV. The Importance of Fairness _____

_____

A. Distributional Fairness _____

_____

B. Procedural Fairness _____

_____

C. Implications for Solving Performance Problems _____

_____

V. The Ultimate Test of Fairness: Downsizing _____

_____

A. Transfers and Layoffs _____

_____

Exercises

1. Return to your managers and ask them about how they solve problems, particularly performance problems. Ask about how they administer both rewards and penalties, and how they handle dismissals.

2. Write an essay outlining your views on managing employees, incorporating what you have learned from the text and what you learned in your interviews.

3. Add your essay to your notebook.

Sources and Further Reading

Folger, R. (2005). The road to fairness and beyond. In K.G. Smith & M.A. Hitt, *Great minds in management* (pp. 55–83). Oxford: Oxford University Press.

Gilliland, S.W., & Schepers, D.H. (2003). Why we do the things we do: A discussion and analysis of determinants of just treatment in layoff implementation decisions. *Human Resource Management Review, 13,* 59–83.

Keer, S. (1975). On the folly of rewarding A while hoping for B. *Academy of Management Journal, 18,* 769–782.

Reb, J., Goldman, B.M., Kray, L.J., & Cropanzano, R. (2006). Different wrongs, different remedies? Reactions to organizational remedies after procedural and interactional injustice. *Personnel Psychology, 59,* 31–64.

Skarlicki, D.P., & Folger, R. (1997). Retaliation in the workplace: The roles of distributive, procedural, and interactional justice. *Journal of Applied Psychology, 82,* 434–443.

—8—

Conclusion

Let's recap what has been covered in the previous chapters.

Introduction

Chapter 1 began by pointing out that almost everyone in an organization has a manager, most of whom are good at what they do, with the possible exception of managing employees, for which they were never trained. As a result, employee management is usually the most stressful part of their jobs. A few find they have a natural talent for it, some learn quickly (but not without sleepless nights), and others adopt expedients—strategies to reduce their anxiety while producing the illusion that they know what they're doing. Review of some of these expedients, and the problems they create, contrasted with what good managers do, reveals six commitments that good managers make that ensures their success.

Good Managers' Six Commitments

- *Leadership.* Good managers commit to actively leading their employees.
- *Expectations.* Good managers commit to understanding their own and their employees' work-related expectations and how they affect behavior.
- *Emotions.* Good managers commit to anticipating the emotions that arise from threatened or violated expectations and to dealing with them constructively.
- *Standards.* Good managers commit to translating their expectations about how employees should behave into clear performance standards.
- *Problems.* Good managers commit to carefully evaluating the problems that arise when their own and their employees' expectations are not met.
- *Solutions.* Good managers commit to solving problems that arise from unmet expectations promptly, fairly, and effectively.

Each of these six commitments was examined in Chapters 2 through 7.

Leadership

Chapter 2 began by defining a unit as a manager and the employees who report directly to him or her and how that unit can be viewed as a mini-enterprise within the larger organization. This view is important because it means that as the manager of a mini-enterprise, you have many of the same responsibilities (and opportunities) that the leader of a large organization has. Primary among them is the responsibility to lead your unit rather than merely maintaining it by serving as a conduit and "enforcer" for higher management. Leadership requires you to take an active role in formulating the unit's vision, delineating the consequent goals, and designing and implementing a plan for attaining those goals. Of course, this must involve your employees, both because the outcomes will substantially affect them and because they will more willingly accept and work toward a vision and goals they helped formulate.

Leadership also requires you to understand the cultures of your organization and your unit: the beliefs and values that influence expectations about how employees should be treated, how they should treat each other, and a host of other aspects of their work-lives. If these expectations are met, everything is fine. If they are exceeded, everyone is pleased. If they are threatened or actually violated, there will be negative reactions.

Sometimes the culture is at cross purposes with the way the organization or unit must move in order to survive and prosper, so the culture must change. Because efforts to change the culture almost inevitably threaten or violate expectations derived from its component beliefs and values, employees generally resist. Executed with care, cultural change can be accomplished slowly, as evolution, or quickly, as revolution, each with its own strengths and drawbacks. Either way, cultural change is stressful for everyone involved, and it requires you to be particularly adroit to carry it through successfully. This includes knowing how to function politically with both your employees and higher management.

A Digression about "Playing Politics"

Politicians have given politics a bad name. Rather than the cut-throat, nefarious enterprise that we tend to think of when we hear the word, politics is simply the process by which people negotiate among themselves to find ways of accommodating their mutual needs and ends. Because the word is so laden with negativity, you frequently have to remind yourself that politics really is about negotiation, not about skullduggery. To maintain perspective, it helps if you translate the complaints you hear about workplace politics into statements about negotiation. For example:

- "I'm just no good at playing politics," which translates, "I don't understand the rules by which others in this organization negotiate among themselves."
- "I refuse to play politics," which translates, "I don't want to endure the stresses involved in serious negotiation about important matters. I want my way or I won't play."
- "It was the result of playing politics," which translates, "I regard the negotiated outcome as inequitable or the process as biased."

Note that the operative phrase in these statements is "playing politics," which suggests a rather dirty little game in which the rules are obscure and shifting, everything is up for grabs, and the results are either preordained or in some way sullied.

When people say they aren't good at politics, they usually mean they find it baffling. However, if they have any social skills at all, they in fact have negotiating skills—which is precisely what they need to "play politics." Virtually every social encounter is a negotiation; each party is seeking something and offering something in exchange, and the process of interacting is about determining how much of one will be exchanged for how much of the other. It isn't exactly an economic exchange, although economists probably would argue that it is. There is a good deal of altruism, and we don't always drive a hard bargain. Indeed, research shows that we often seek an equitable compromise in which all parties get all or as much as they can get of whatever they want. The general idea is to work out a way of getting along with each other and providing for each other's needs in a reasonably friendly way.

Workplace politics is merely an extension of our everyday social exchanges, but the range of compromise usually is more limited than in our private lives. Combine this limited range with ambition and some participants are apt to play more aggressively than they otherwise might, and some are apt to cheat. It is this aspect of politics that the rest of us complain about.

Of course, some things aren't negotiable: you don't think human life should be bargained about, although governments do it. You don't think that ethics should be negotiated, although it clearly happens. In general, you feel uncomfortable and somehow demeaned if you are forced to negotiate non-negotiables.

Finally, when outcomes accrue to people who don't deserve them, or when their getting those outcomes results from favoritism or some other way of skirting the rules, both the improper results and the negotiations leading to them are generally regarded as illegitimate. As was said in Chapter 7, corruption can be defined as the illegitimate use of different rules for different people, and corrupt negotiations are almost universally detested (unless you're the one who profits—in which case it doesn't always seem so bad).

Even when you understand that politics is negotiation, you sometimes find yourself dreading getting involved or regretting having been involved. Usually this is because one or both parties approached the negotiation under false pretenses—real negotiation wasn't the purpose of the interaction at all. This happens when one or another party:

- Is intent on winning, not on finding a mutually acceptable agreement;
- Is intent on merely going through the motions, not on reaching any agreement;
- Is intent on inflicting harm on the other person, so there could never be an agreement.

If one party insists on winning, there is no point in negotiating—the whole point of negotiating is to find a mutually acceptable solution. The only way one party can be sure of prevailing is if the other party is negotiating from a position of weakness—if it hasn't anything of interest to offer or if it lacks the power to insist on genuine negotiation. In that case, the more powerful party can do as it likes; it doesn't need to negotiate. We'll discuss power in a moment.

When one party is merely going through the motions, pretending to negotiation, it usually means that a deal has been worked out on a higher level of the organization and the sham negotiation is merely window dressing. For example, if your bosses have decided that your prize employee is to be transferred, your boss may try to soothe your feelings by pretending to negotiate—perhaps even giving you something to make you feel better. But you know it isn't a negotiation; you've been steamrolled, and no amount of well-intended pretense is going to help (although it may permit you to save face in the eyes of your employees).

Sometimes what appears to be a negotiation isn't. If the purpose of the interaction is for one party to humiliate, intimidate, or otherwise harm the other, negotiation isn't the issue. When a manager asks an employee, "What do you think we should do about your poor performance?" it may look like the opportunity for a negotiation, but it probably is just a game in which the employee is supposed to guess what the manager already has in mind. "Negotiations" about pay often are like this—just the trappings of an exchange, not the real thing. And the underdog in this ritual comes away feeling just a bit diminished, as though he or she been treated condescendingly.

People who claim to hate politics often do so because they think their opponents are conspiring against them and/or their unit. Of course, conspiracies happen, but the more complicated they appear to be, the less likely they are to actually exist; most people aren't well enough organized to plan and implement an authentic conspiracy. Conspiracies are complex and hard to coordinate, and they are far less frequent than the movies or TV would lead us to think.

Coalitions are far more common. These occur when your opponents work together to thwart you. They're too straightforward to be conspiracies; you're simply being ganged-up on, and it is a legitimate tactic in negotiations. Coalitions are formed when your opponents think you are not negotiating in good faith or that your needs and wants are too extravagant. When you encounter a coalition, you should ask yourself what prompted its formation; perhaps you should reexamine your motives and reassess your real needs.

Expectations

Chapter 3 began with an explanation of what workplace expectations are and what they do. They derive from one's own beliefs and values, together with the organization's and the unit's cultural beliefs and values, as well as from workplace experiences. They take the form of scenarios that describe what should happen in a given situation; consequently, their violation leads to both emotions and to action. Violation means that what might happen or what actually has happened is significantly discrepant from what should happen (your expectations). "Might happen" produces a threat and "has happened" produces a violation. Action consists of trying to escape (which makes the threat or violation irrelevant) or attempts to remove the threat or eliminate the violation. Expectations that are particularly important, and therefore are especially sensitive to threats or violations, are called "hot buttons," and it is wise to know what yours are so people cannot manipulate you.

When expectations become moral obligations, we call them ethics. The difficulty with ethics—in fact, the difficulty with all expectations—is knowing when they apply. Rather than trusting individual employees to decide for themselves, many organizations have adopted codes of ethics or codes of conduct that describe dangerous situations, the prescribed behavior, and the penalties for not complying. It is a good idea for units to have a pared-down code of conduct, tailored to their specific needs.

Just as managers have expectations about how their employees should behave, employees have expectations about how managers should behave and about their professional image. Because the manager frequently represents the unit both within the organization and outside of it, employees don't want you to embarrass them.

A Digression about Meeting Volunteers' Expectations

Perhaps, of all the people you will ever manage, volunteers arrive with the highest and most specific expectations; they believe in what you are doing and want to learn more about it. Whether they are students, retirees, or anyone in between, they are willing to work for little or nothing in exchange for experience. Too often they are disappointed.

Most organizations violate volunteers' expectations because they don't think through what they want volunteers to do and how they are going to manage them while they do it. You've got to plan ahead:

- Figure out what the volunteer program is to accomplish for the organization or unit.
- Devote resources to the program to make sure it is viable.
- Make a regular employee responsible for overall coordination of the volunteer program, arranging flexible schedules and work assignments.
- Create an orientation program in which new volunteers learn about the organization and a briefer version to orient them to the unit in which they will be working.
- Train employees to work with volunteers; they're not servants nor should they be given make-work projects just to keep them busy.
- Match each volunteer's goals with the unit's needs in making assignments.
- Write job descriptions so everyone will know what each volunteer will be doing and to whom they report.
- Provide adequate workspace and resources to help volunteers do their tasks comfortably and effectively—and, if possible, provide a parking space; after all, you're not paying them.
- Make sure volunteers understand how the tasks they are given contribute to the unit's efforts; help them achieve their goal of learning about the organization, the unit, and what you do.
- Evaluate volunteers' performance and give them feedback.
- Honor volunteers' contributions by saying thanks and integrating them as much as possible into the social aspects of the unit's daily routine.
- Listen carefully to volunteers' complaints; if their expectations are not met, they will leave.
- Conduct exit interviews.

It is so easy for a well-intended volunteer program to degenerate, leaving previously enthused volunteers hostile and disillusioned. For example, a newly retired couple of my acquaintance answered a call for volunteers by a governmental agency that does anthropological research. They did so out of a desire to do something worthwhile for the community and with the expectation that they would learn a bit about anthropological research. The orientation session was informative and made it look like their expectations would be met. However, the enthusiastic consultant who conducted the orientation left immediately after it was over and was never seen nor heard from again. They were assigned to a very nice woman who, it turned out, was more concerned about her imminent retirement than about volunteers. She turned them over to another woman, who set them to work sorting approximately 40,000 small pieces of paper on the basis of a cluster of nearly illegible numbers scribbled on each paper. Their repeated questions about what the numbers meant, what the papers were, and why they were sorting them received only sketchy answers, as though they might not be bright enough to handle more detail. After weeks of work, they finished the sorting task, hoping the next task would better meet their expectations. But there was no next task. Instead, their supervisor took them around asking people if they needed help, to which the usual reply was, "Maybe next time," but nothing was ever ready when they arrive the next time. After a few weeks of this, the supervisor stopped showing up. Finally, feeling like fools, they could see that things weren't going to improve and that they weren't going to learn anything about anthropologic research. So, they resigned. As you might expect, they never heard anything from the agency, not even an acknowledgment of their resignation.

A Digression about the Generality of Expectations

Expectations form the core of human experience, in the workplace and everywhere else. Every story you ever read, ever saw on TV or in a movie, or were ever told in the course of a conversation revolved around threats to or violations of expectations; the crux of everything important to us is how our expectations are or are not met, and the resulting emotions and actions.

Expectations aren't just the elements of your conscious mental life; they are essential to virtually every aspect of what you do. Without being aware of it, every time you take a step, you do so in the expectation that the sidewalk or floor will remain solid and that your step will propel you safely forward. When your expectation is violated, when something causes you to stumble, your reaction is both surprise and annoyance—you often see people looking disapprovingly at the pebble or crack that caused them to trip. Each time you reach for an object, it is in the expectation that your motions will result in grasping it. If the expectation is violated, if you misjudge the distance and knock it over, you react with exasperation—which is mild anger. Virtually everything you do is based on the expectation that it will produce a predictable, valued result, and you usually are right. And, each time you're right, it goes unnoticed because, after all, it was expected. It is only when things go wrong, when expectations are violated, that you pay much attention to them.

Emotions

Chapter 4 continued the discussion of emotional responses to threats to or violations of expectations. Managers have to learn to distinguish between drama and trauma, both their employees' and their own. Drama merely needs to play itself out; letting off steam. Trauma usually requires you to do something because it can have concrete repercussions.

Fear is a reaction to threats and can lead to leaving, hunkering down (which is a form of escape), or attempting to remove the threat. Sometimes the attempts to thwart the threat are effective, and sometimes they simply create more problems. Fear motivates, but it sometimes narrows one's thinking about what to do.

Anger is a general reaction to violated expectations, but is particularly evidenced when there is a discrepancy between how one expects to be treated by one's boss and coworkers and how one is actually treated. Unexpressed anger helps the angry person know how important the violation is to him or her; expressed anger lets everyone know. Expressed anger is a form of bullying that attempts to elicit appeasement from the person who is the object of the anger—appeasement that will remove the violation and alleviate the anger. Explanations and apologies can both reduce anger and, to some degree, appease it. Extreme anger becomes hatred and can lead to violence. Managers are, of course, obligated to protect their employees from violence by anticipating and trying to prevent it whenever possible.

Stress is anxiety resulting from real or perceived lack of control. Stress junkies embrace stress as the badge of being important and having high-pressure jobs. Try not to encourage them.

Romance, lust, and love are a workplace problem because they cause coworkers concern about whether the persons involved receive special treatment or in some other way obtain advantages that the coworkers don't have. Managers are wise to include the rules about workplace romance in the unit's code of conduct.

A Digression about Frustration

It is not uncommon for workers to experience frustration, which is a mixture of anger and stress—where the former is a reaction to unmet expectations and the latter is a reaction to a lack of control. Frustration results from real or perceived powerlessness, when someone threatens or violates your expectations and prevents you from thwarting the threat or correcting the violation. Because of the hierarchical power structure in most organizations, powerlessness usually has no immediate remedy, other than quitting. The immediate question is how to handle the frustration itself, followed by the question of how to eliminate it. When you are feeling frustrated, you should answer the following questions:

- Who is the source of your frustration? Identify the person or persons who threaten/violate your expectations and make you powerless to respond.
- How are you currently dealing with your frustration?
- What are the consequences for you and for your unit of what you are doing to deal with your frustration?
- How might you work out your frustration in a more constructive way?
- What can be done to eliminate your frustration?

For example, suppose your employees are pressuring you to obtain equipment the unit needs to do its work more efficiently. You meet with your boss, but when he hears the price, he immediately stops listening and simply tells you that the old equipment will have to do. You think for a moment and then request permission to apply to higher management's equipment procurement committee. He refuses your request because he doesn't think you'll be successful and he doesn't want to bother with the large amount of work the application would require.

The next day your employees ask about what happened in your meeting with your boss, and you rudely snap that it is out of your hands and you don't want to hear any more about it. Later, lying in bed and staring at the ceiling, you ask yourself the questions listed above and realize that your frustration results from being caught between your employees and your boss, and powerless to do anything to resolve things. Your frustration has led you to be rude to your employees, snapping at them and making them feel as powerless and frustrated as you feel. You spend the rest of the night trying to think of creative solutions to your dilemma.

Standards

Chapter 5 examined how you, as manager, translate your expectations into standards for guiding and evaluating your employees' performance. Because expectations are about what should happen, they necessarily are standards against which we measure our own and others' behavior. As workplace standards, however, they must be explicit, thorough, and communicated clearly so employees will know precisely what you want. Presuming that they accept your standards as reasonable and legitimate, employees use them to guide their behavior, expecting to be evaluated in light of them. Some standards are general (commitment and conduct) and some are specific (job and task). They are for your unit, for individual employees, and for teams.

Standards are useful only insofar as compliance with them produces good consequences. Because your standards are used for performance evaluations, employees expect that meeting them will produce rewards: formal rewards like money, status, or opportunities, and informal rewards like approval and recognition. They expect that failure to meet them will produce penalties: withholding of rewards, discipline, dismissal. Of course, those expectations presume that you have the power to meet them.

A Digression about the Nature of Power

You have the power to set and enforce standards because it is granted to you by the organization, called position power, and because it is granted to you by the employees themselves, called personal power. The organization grants you position power by defining standard-setting as part of your job and backing your enforcement decisions. Your employees grant you personal power because they trust you to use it wisely. Their trust is based on their belief that you have your job in the first place because of your ability and experience. If you show yourself to be unqualified or if they were to learn that you got your job through illegitimate means, such as favoritism or cheating or error, your personal power would evaporate, leaving only position power, greatly diminishing your ability to set and enforce standards.

Although it has become politically incorrect to talk about it, your position power and personal power are augmented by a goodly portion of old fashioned coercive power—the iron hand within the velvet glove. Coercive power induces employees to meet your standards even if they are disinclined to do so. It derives from the organization's rules and employees' anticipation (threat) of being penalized for breaking them, from your ability to control the distribution of work-related resources and employees' anticipation of losing their share if they fail to comply, and from a culturally accepted obligation for employees to comply with their manager's directives and their anticipation of both coworkers' disapproval and their own guilty feelings if they fail to do so. Taken together, position power, personal power, and coercive power give you a considerable amount of authority. But you have it only so long as the organization and your employees are willing to grant it to you, so care must be taken to exercise it prudently.

Problems

In Chapter 6, we saw that threatened or violated expectations and standards constitute problems that you must address if the unit is to succeed. The discussion focused on how to make sure you keep from jumping to conclusions and incorrectly assigning blame as you strive to understand performance problems —failures to meet your standards. First you must figure out (evaluate) if there actually is a problem and, if so, how serious it is. Then, if it exists and is serious, you must figure out (attribute) what caused it. There are two classes of causes, person causes and situational causes, and your job is to figure out which kind is causing the current problem and then fix it.

You have two tools: asking questions and causal analysis. Employees' answers to your questions help you decide about the existence and seriousness of the problem. Causal analysis uses these same answers to help you decide if the problem's cause is the situation or a person. Problems may be a result of what you do or don't do, primarily if you fail to live up to any of the six commitments listed in the Introduction and discussed in each of the next six chapters. They also result from what your employees do: impaired productivity, insubordination, annoying behavior, and adverse reactions to diversity.

A Digression about Sexual Harassment

Sexual harassment is a particularly difficult and dangerous problem for every organization. Moreover, it isn't just your employees you must worry about. The organization, as well as you personally, is at risk if you do anything that can be legally shown to constitute sexual harassment. Even if the legal definition isn't met, the expenses of mounting a defense can be considerable.

I presume that you understand that harassment of any kind is unacceptable and that you do not intentionally harass your employees, men or women. Still, you must be alert to the fact that what may not seem like harassment to you may very much seem like it to someone else. Furthermore, what to you might be a funny joke or wisecrack may be regarded by others as offensive, hostile, and intimidating. This is as true of jokes about men as it is jokes about women; jokes involving sex and gender should not be part of your repertoire.

One way to avoid doing things that might be interpreted as harassment is to avoid becoming overly friendly with any particular employee. It is better to err on the side of formality than on the side of intimacy—you're their manager, not their pal. The way to discourage harassment among your employees is to make sure that the unit's behavioral code includes a section describing what constitutes sexual harassment and making it clear that both the organization and the unit disapprove of it, that disciplinary action will be taken when it occurs, and that employees have the right to raise harassment claims and expect results. The code also should include instructions about how to make a claim. Your human resources office, or a lawyer, can give you a full description of the responsibilities and legal issues involved in sexual harassment.

As a manager, you must be aware of the potential for sexual harassment in your unit and you must stop it if it occurs. The most common way of learning about an occurrence is by being told by the person who alleges to have been harassed or by their coworkers. Any allegation requires an immediate response, because it's the right thing to do and because the law requires it. If you have a human resources department, the problem should be reported to them; they presumably know how to deal with it. If you are on your own, you must look into the charges and do your best to be fair to everyone involved.

It is important to remember that the alleged harasser has rights too. You must not assume guilt simply because there has been an accusation. As with every other problem, you must talk with everybody involved so you can understand what actually occurred. Then you must take appropriate action.

The point is to prevent harassment in the first place, and to stop it immediately if it occurs. If this can be done through diplomacy, satisfying both the accused and the accuser, that is fine. If it requires transfers or discipline or firing, so be it, but allow the person the opportunity to appeal your decision to your boss or higher. Always keep in mind that you are on thin ice legally; if you don't solve the problem to the complainant's satisfaction, you may have to deal with the Equal Employment Opportunity Commission (EEOC) or a lawsuit. The person you punish may sue too.

Your best strategy is:

- Keep your boss and other authorities informed and listen to their advice.
- Bring in the human resources specialists, if you have them, as soon as you can. Cooperate with them throughout their inquiry.
- If you don't have access to a specialist, be as objective and as thorough as possible throughout your investigation of the allegation.
- Have a disinterested person observe the whole process to make sure you do it right.
- Keep detailed records of everything that happens and everything you do.
- Don't make all the decisions yourself. If there is a disciplinary committee, use it. If not, perhaps you should convene one.
- Have legal counsel from the beginning.

Solutions

Chapter 7 continued the discussion of problems began in Chapter 6, turning to how to solve them. When the situation causes the problem, you must change the situation. Situational causes usually involve poorly designed tasks, jobs, work settings, social codes, and/or incentive systems. In each case the solution is to think through the demands and to redesign to fit those demands. Vague, inefficient tasks, poorly thought through job specifications, impractical and inefficient workspace configurations, and incentive systems that fail to encourage the desired behavior all can be repaired with a bit of careful thought and appropriate action.

People causes are more complicated than situational causes, but the solution is much the same; you have to make changes. Your arsenal for changing employees consists of talking with them about how their behavior is causing the problem and working with them to solve it, remediation, reassignment, discipline, and dismissal—each of which is an escalation in the seriousness of your action. Through it all, however, you must strive to appear fair and to actually be fair. There are two kinds of fairness in problem-solving, procedural and distributional. This means that the procedures must be fair and the distribution of rewards or penalties must be fair. Downsizing is the ultimate test of fairness.

A Digression about the Art of Thanking

The word "thanks" is among the most frequently used words in the English language, largely because the word can convey different messages. Because it can mean different things, it is important to know what message you're sending when you thank an employee for good performance.

Thanks as *recognition* means that the employee did his or her job well. It does not imply that you, the unit, or the organization are indebted to him or her, because the level of performance was within the definition of the job, the high end of the definition, perhaps, but still what can be reasonably expected of a person holding that job and doing what is expected. The implicit message is, "You did your job, for which you are paid, and I am merely recognizing that you did it well." The explicit message is, "Thanks for doing your job so well. It is employees like you who make this organization (or unit) work." This kind of thanks requires nothing more from you.

Thanks as *gratitude* means that you, as the employee's manager, feel indebted to him or her for performing at or beyond the upper limits of the job requirements. The implicit message is, "I owe you one." The explicit message is, "Thanks for the extra effort. I'm sure we all are indebted to you for helping the organization (unit) in this important way." This kind of thanks requires you, in your capacity as his or her manager, to repay the extra effort with a little special treatment somewhere down the line. Perhaps the employee might be granted some favor that otherwise would not have been granted, but once that happens the debt is paid and you should make it clear that there will be no further repayment.

Thanks as *promise* means that you, representing the organization or unit, promise that the extra effort will be rewarded in a concrete and enduring way. Usually this consists of a bonus, pay raise, or promotion, either now or in the near future. The implicit and explicit messages are the same, "Thanks for the extra effort, and the organization (unit) will reward you for it."

The art of thanking employees lies in conveying the correct implicit message by careful wording of the explicit message. If you are too effusive in thanking someone for merely doing their job well, you may create expectations for future favors or concrete rewards when, in fact, you have no intention of delivering. By carelessly leading a good employee to expect more than you intend to deliver, you plant the seeds of future conflict when those expectations go unmet. In doing so, you turn a good employee into a disappointed and dissatisfied employee—all because you sent the wrong message by the way you expressed thanks.

A Digression about You

You can't really hope to change other people's behavior if you don't have your own house in order—the old dictum "Do as I say, not as I do," doesn't work. First of all, you need to build a good working relationship with your boss. You must make sure you understand his or her expectations and standards for your behavior. If they seem unrealistic or wrong, you must negotiate changes that both of you can live with. Then you must seek clear feedback about your performance relative to those standards. Remember, your boss is only human, so be reasonable—you can live with being judged a little too harshly sometimes, a little too laxly at other times. Your boss has more things to worry about than just you, so be as independent as you can without jeopardizing your relationship.

Second, independence requires you to monitor your own performance. This begins with setting personal performance goals that are congruent with your boss's standards and that are compatible with the organization's rules, culture, and vision. You and your unit are part of the organization's thrust toward its vision, and you must contribute to that thrust or you are irrelevant.

Third, you must manage your own work effectively. This means learning to manage your time, for instance, managing face-to-face, telephone, and electronic access so you have time to keep up with paperwork—and time to think. It means learning to communicate effectively with your boss, other unit managers, and your employees—perhaps seeking a coach if you need one. It means learning to observe your own actions as objectively as possible—hoping things are going well isn't good enough. It means learning from your successes as well as your errors. It means scolding yourself for doing poorly, and moving on. It means rewarding yourself for your successes—even when you're the only one who knows there was a success. It means focusing on opportunities rather than obstacles. In short, it means thinking about yourself and your behavior with the same clarity you attempt to achieve when thinking about your employees and their behavior.

A Parting Word

In Chapter 3 we said that the Manager's Golden Rule is "Do unto your employees as you would have your boss do unto you." This is because your employees expect of you exactly the same things you expect of your boss. Like you, they expect their manager to be a leader, to understand their workplace expectations and emotions and to deal with them honestly and constructively, to set clear standards for what is expected of them and the unit, to avoid jumping to conclusions about blame when standards aren't met, and to solve the problem promptly, fairly, and effectively. Fundamental to your success as an employee manager is your determination to become the kind of manager that you would like to have as your manager.

Summary

To ensure mastery of the material in this chapter, summarize it for yourself by filling in this topic outline.

I. Introduction _____

_____

   A. Good Managers' Six Commitments _____

_____

II. Leadership _____

_____

   A. A Digression about "Playing Politics" _____

_____

III. Expectations _____

_____

A. A Digression about Meeting Volunteers' Expectations _____

_____

B. A Digression about the Generality of Expectations _____

_____

IV. Emotions _____

_____

A. A Digression about Frustration _____

_____

V. Standards

_____

A. A Digression about the Nature of Power _____

_____

VI. Problems _____

_____

A. A Digression about Sexual Harassment _____

_____

VII. Solutions _____

_____

A. A Digression about the Art of Thanking _____

_____

B. A Digression about You _____

_____

VIII. A Parting Word_____

_____

Exercises

1. Return to your three managers and ask them about their views on workplace politics, managing volunteers, frustration and powerlessness, power, sexual harassment, and personal work habits as an element in career advancement.

2. Write a short essay summarizing their views and adding your own.

3. Add this essay to your notebook.

4. Review all of your essays and write a final essay that describes your personal viewpoint about managing employees.

Sources and Further Reading

Anderson, D.V. (1985). *Illusions of power.* New York: Praeger.

Beach, L.R. (2005). *Leadership and the art of change.* Thousand Oaks, CA: Sage.

Fisher, R., Patton, B.M., & Ury, W.L. (1992). *Getting to yes: Negotiating agreement without giving in* (2nd ed.). Boston: Houghton Mifflin.

Appendix
An Example of a
Culture Inventory

Big Bank's Retail Division

The purpose of this inventory is to permit you to describe the culture of Big Bank's Retail Division—not what it should be but what it actually is.

Step 1: Turn to Part I of the Inventory. Begin by dividing 100 points among the five cultural norms that focus on employees to reflect their relative priority in the Retail Division's culture. Limit your thinking to *only* the five cultural norms listed in Part I of the Inventory. Give more of the 100 points to the norms that have a relatively higher priority and fewer of the 100 points to the norms that have a relatively lower priority, writing your answers in the blanks on the left. (Because the priorities are relative to one another, and you must limit your thinking to the five norms in Part I of the Inventory, the points *must* add up to *100* across the five norms.)

Step 2: Now do the same thing for Parts II and III.

Step 3: Finally, in Part IV of the Inventory, divide 100 points among Parts I, II, and III, treating each of them as a unitary cluster of norms, in order to indicate the relative priorities of the five clusters in the Retail Division's culture.

Part I. Big Bank's Retail Division Culture: Focus on Employees

Priority

_____   **Caring:** Valuing the contributions of each employee and embracing diversity.

_____   **Learning & Development:** Recognizing the responsibility of managers and employees to promote personal growth by increasing the skills and knowledge necessary to serve customers and to create a challenging and viable career path.

_____   **Motivation:** Promoting a "sales organization" mentality through compensation, recognition, responsibility, and accountability.

_____   **Communication:** Promoting openness and a free flow of information throughout the division by clearly stating the vision, values, goals, strategies, competitive advantages, and disadvantages.

_____   **Empowerment:** Encouraging "ownership," creativity, innovation, enjoyment, responsible risk taking, and responsive decision making.

_____   **Total:** Sum must equal 100 points.

Part II. Big Bank's Retail Division Culture: Focus on Customers

Priority

_____   **Respect:** Putting customers' needs first and foremost by responding quickly and creatively to those needs while treating customers as we would like to be treated.

_____   **Relationships:** Deepening the total relationship with customers in order to serve them better.

_____   **Technology:** Increasing convenient delivery of multiple services to customers through user-friendly technological innovation.

_____   **Team Selling:** Working with our partners throughout Big Bank to provide a broad array of products to meet our customers' needs, with all team members committed to selling.

_____   **Expansion:** Retaining and deepening our relationship with our present customers while actively pursuing new customers through sales that serve their unique needs.

_____   **Total:** Sum must equal 100 points.

Part III. Big Bank's Retail Division Culture: Focus on the Community

Priority

_____   **Integrity:** Demonstrating high moral and ethical business standards.

_____   **Leadership:** Improving the community through provision of superior financial services and leadership in the community.

_____   **Responsiveness:** Building a strong community banking presence through accountable, prompt, local decision making.

_____   **Image:** Associating the Big Bank brand with activities that have a positive impact on the quality of our community.

_____   **Participation:** Encouraging employee involvement in community organizations and activities.

_____   **Total:** Sum must equal 100 points.

Part IV. All Three Parts Together

Big Bank's Retail Division Culture: Overall

Priority

_____   **Part I. Focus on Employees:** Caring, Learning & Development, Motivation, Communication, Empowerment

_____   **Part II. Focus on Customers:** Respect, Relationships, Technology, Team Selling, Expansion

_____   **Part III. Focus on the Community:** Integrity, Leadership, Responsiveness, Image, Participation

_____   **Total:** Sum must equal 100 points.

Part V. For the Manager:
Computation of the Results

To derive an individual respondent's view of the relative salience of the fifteen norms in the unit's culture, first convert all of the points to decimal numbers (for example, 5 points become .05). Then, multiply the decimal numbers corresponding to the points allotted to each of the three clusters in Part IV of the Inventory by the decimal numbers corresponding to the points allotted to each of the five paragraphs corresponding to that cluster in Parts II and III. The resulting fifteen products will sum to approximately 1.00. Multiply each product by 100 to get rid of decimal numbers; the resulting set of fifteen numbers represents the relative salience of each of the fifteen norms on the list. For multiple respondents, means of these numbers can be computed across respondents for each of the fifteen norms to yield a more stable measure of the unit's culture. The variance associated with these means indicates the degree of disagreement among the respondents. The mean relative salience of each of the fifteen norms is best summarized in a bar graph.

Index

About the Author

Lee Roy Beach is McClelland Professor Emeritus of Management and Policy at the Eller College of Business, University of Arizona, Tucson. He received his Ph.D. in Psychology from the University of Colorado and began his professional career in human factors research for the U.S. Navy, followed by service at the Office of Naval Research. After leaving the navy, he completed two years of postdoctoral work in the psychology of decision making at the University of Michigan before joining the Cognitive and the Organizational Psychology programs at the University of Washington, where he moved from assistant to full professor, served as Chair of the Psychology Department, received the Alumni Award for Distinguished Teaching, was named Professor of the Year for the State of Washington and Bronze Medallist for National Professor of the Year, received the Feldman Award for research and was named to the University Teaching Academy. He has been a Visiting Scholar at Cambridge (England) and Leiden (the Netherlands) universities and a Visiting Professor of Business at the University of Chicago. After joining the Eller College at Arizona, he was named Professor of the Year, served as Vice Dean, and taught graduate and executive education courses while engaged in extensive research and consulting. He has served as a Fellow of the American Psychological Association and the American Psychological Society, and is the author of over 125 scholarly articles and 7 books on organizational behavior and decision making, the latest of which are *The Psychology of Decision Making* and *Leadership and the Art of Change.*